Polish Folktales and Folklore

World Folklore Advisory Board

Polish Folktales and Folklore

Retold by Michał Malinowski and Anne Pellowski

World Folklore Series

LIBRARIES
UNLIMITED
A Member of the Greenwood Publishing Group

Westport, Connecticut • London

Library of Congress Cataloging-in-Publication Data

Polish folktales and folklore / retold by Michał Malinowski and Anne Pellowski.
   p. cm. — (World folklore series)
 Includes bibliographical references and index.
 ISBN 978-1-59158-723-1 (alk. paper)
 1. Tales—Poland. I. Malinowski, Michał. II. Pellowski, Anne.
 GR195.P65   2009
 398.209438—dc22   2008028655

British Library Cataloguing in Publication Data is available.

Library of Congress Catalog Card Number: 2008028655
ISBN: 978-1-59158-723-1

First published in 2009

Libraries Unlimited, 88 Post Road West, Westport, CT 06881
A Member of the Greenwood Publishing Group, Inc.
www.lu.com

Printed in the United States of America

The paper used in this book complies with the
Permanent Paper Standard issued by the National
Information Standards Organization (Z39.48–1984).

10 9 8 7 6 5 4 3 2 1

The publisher has done its best to make sure the instructions and/or recipes in this book are correct.
However, users should apply judgment and experience when preparing recipes, especially parents
and teachers working with young people. The publisher accepts no responsibility for the outcome of
any recipe included in this volume.

To my first storytellers: my mother, who introduced tales that led me to the path of goodness and wisdom; my father, for sharing stories that opened my eyes to beauty; and my Aunt Domicela, who taught me how to discover the story hidden in the smallest object.

Michał Malinowski

To the memory of my grandparents, parents, aunts, uncles, and cousins who shared their folklore, and to my nieces, nephews, grand-nieces, and grand-nephews, with whom I have had so much pleasure in passing it on.

Anne Pellowski

CONTENTS

Part 1: General Introduction to Poland

Part 2: Food, Games, Riddles, and Nursery Rhymes

Part 3: Local Legends

Part 4: Animal Tales

Part 5: Magic Tales

Part 6: Chain Chants and Cumulative Tales

Part 7: Humorous Tales

Part 8: Why Tales

Part 9: Religious Legends

Part 10: Supernatural Creatures

PREFACE

A number of Polish folktale books have been published in English, but most have included only one type: legends, historical tales, animal tales, or what are known as magical fairy tales. It was our goal to include all of these types, as well as other forms of folk literature and arts, so that the reader could have a sampling in one volume. We wished to pay special attention to the legends found in the earliest chronicles, among them Gallus Anonymous, Kadlubek, Baszko, and Dlugosz.

There are more than fifty tales included here, loosely organized by type. In addition to the legends from medieval sources, we attempted to include a translation of at least one tale from each of the collections published in the nineteenth century, as well as a number collected in the early part of the twentieth. About ten are from oral sources given directly to the authors.

The nursery rhymes are included because they often provide young children with their first inkling of sequence that leads to story. Riddles, even today, are a form of folklore that every child experiences, most often in purely oral form. Because the riddles of today are so different from those of the past, it seemed appropriate to recall some of the commonly known early riddles.

The translations of the tales were provided in rough form by Michał Malinowski and polished by Anne Pellowski. If the tales were adapted in some way, this is noted in the Sources section. The translations of the nursery rhymes were done solely by Anne Pellowski.

ACKNOWLEDGMENTS

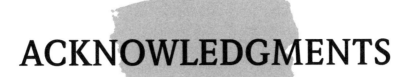

Both of the authors wish to acknowledge the pioneering work done by Oskar Kolberg in the nineteenth century and Julian Krzyzanowski in the twentieth. Kolberg's extensive work in recording the folk songs, folktales, and other folklore of nearly all the peoples of Poland has been of enormous help in locating material for this book. The work of Krzyzanowski in classifying Polish folklore has also proved to be of inestimable value.

Anne Pellowski thanks the reference librarians and staff of the Winona Public Library, especially Robin Youngerman and Susan Steckel, for their extraordinary help in arranging interlibrary loans of many items needed for checking bibliographic entries.

Special thanks to Agnieszka Kadej for checking the diacritical marks in the Sources and Bibliography sections. Thanks also to Jeffrey Garrett of Northwestern University and Oksana Kraus of the Cleveland Public Library for helping to locate copies of certain texts, and to Marilyn Berg Iarusso, formerly of the New York Public Library, for her warm hospitality while checking numerous sources in New York.

Michał Malinowski thanks the following storytellers for sharing their tales: Jozef Budz, Piotr Makowski, Cecilia Slapek, and many other persons in Mazovia. Thanks to Anna Kierkosz and the Mazovian Center of Culture and Arts for financing field work in the region. Great thanks to the people who sparked my interest and helped me develop methods of collecting folklore, especially the following professors: Deborah Foster from Harvard University, Henry Glassie from Indiana University, Machiko Kusahara from Waseda University, and Zofia Rosinska from Warsaw University. Thanks also to French writer and storyteller Muriel Bloch, Canadian storyteller Dan Yashinsky, and Bulgarian folklore researcher Nadia Georgieva for sharing their perceptions of the folktale and its place in modern life. The sharing of ideas with many Polish folklore enthusiasts, especially Remigiusz Hanaj, Katarzyna Brzozowska and Maria Pomianowska, was influential.

NOTE ABOUT DIACRITICAL MARKS

Because this book is intended for English-language readers, in the main sections of the book and in the index the English spelling of personal and place names and titles is used in almost every case. Diacritical marks are used only if necessary to distinguish one name from another. An exception is Mr. Malinowski's first name. In the "Sources" and "Bibliography" all diacritical marks have been used, so that the reader needing the correct spelling of the original Polish will be able to find it.

MAPS OF POLAND

Geographical Region of Poland

Ethnographical Map of Poland

PART 1

General Introduction to Poland

THE LAND

Poland has an area of just over 120,000 square miles and is the seventh largest country in Europe. It stretches from the Baltic Sea in the north to the Carpathian Mountains in the south for approximately 400 miles. From the border with Russia and Belarus along the Bug River in the east to the border with Germany along the Oder River in the west, it is approximately 420 miles across.

About 75 percent of Poland is flat and at or below sea level. Along the Baltic Sea is the coastal plain. This includes the Masurian Lake District, the Kaszubian Lake District, and the Pomeranian Lake District. The largest lakes are in the Masurian, to the east of the city of Olsztyn. There are also many small forests in these areas.

The central Polish plain has some hills but is mostly noted for the valleys on each side of the Vistula (Wisla), Oder (Odra), Warta, and Bug Rivers. One small mountain range, the Holy Cross, is located in south central Poland. Within the area are many small towns and traditional villages. The central plain of Poland also has a number of upland areas that contain many caves and interesting rock formations.

Perhaps the most unusual part of the central Polish plain lies on the eastern border, just southeast of the city of Bialystok. This is the great primeval forest of Bialowieza, the last surviving forest of this size and character in Europe. Slightly less than one half is in Poland; the other part is in Belarus. It contains the last herds of European bison and an early type of horse, the tarpan, about the size of a pony. There are also many forms of flora and fauna found nowhere else in Europe.

The southern part of Poland is mostly mountainous. The Sudeten Range in the southwest stretches along the northern border of the Czech Republic for several hundred miles. The Carpathian Range, shared with Slovakia and the Ukraine, is the longest range. The mountains run in parallel rows and are often called Beskidy or the Beskids. The Tatras, really a part of the Carpathians, are found in the extreme south. Beginning at Zakopane, they stretch down into Slovakia like two butterfly wings and contain the highest peak in Poland, Mount Rysy, which is about 2,500 meters (8,300 feet) high.

LANGUAGES

Polish is a branch of the west Slavic languages, all of which are descended from the Indo-Iranian language family. Most of the languages of Europe are also descended from this family. They branched out over time and developed in various ways. The Slavic languages developed grammars distinctly different from the other Indo-European languages. They have the most elaborate verb forms.

Polish probably had reached its basic form by the tenth century. It retained quite a number of Persian words (but in Polonized form) and added words taken from Latin, German, French, Hungarian, and a number of other languages. Many scholars estimate that just over half of the words in the largest unabridged Polish dictionaries (about 200,000 words) are of purely Slavic origin.

Virtually all Poles speak a form of standard Polish, but there are pockets of people who speak a dialect as well. The Kaszubians and Slovincians in the north speak forms of Slavonic languages that are closely related to Polish but are now classified as languages in their own right. In the border areas some people's primary language is German, Czech, Slovak, Lithuanian, Ukrainian, or another language, but generally they are bilingual, speaking Polish as well.

THE PEOPLE

Most of the people living in Poland today are descended from the Slavic tribes that were present at the time Poland was first identified as a political unit around 860 C.E.. The group that gave its name to the country, the Polanie ("field dwellers"), lived mostly on the central plain. Other groups listed in the early records of Poland are the Masurians, Kaszubians, Slovincians and other Pomeranians, Slezanie (who later became the Silesians), Vistulans, and Warmians. Many of these groups still exist, living in tightly knit families in various parts of Poland. They are almost all descended from even older Slavonic tribes.

These groups came from eastern Europe, what is now the Middle East, and Asia, and it is likely they had extensive contacts with Scythians and other peoples from Persia, because there are numerous Persian loan words in Polish. There was certainly intermarriage between 4000 B.C.E. and 1000 C.E. between these tribes and Germanic tribes such as the Goths. There is even evidence of Celtic intermarriage and influence, especially in the southern part of Poland, known as Galicia, which is generally thought to mean "land of the Gaels."

Centuries later various armies or invading groups that either passed though Poland or stayed and ruled there for a time also added to the mix. This was probably true during some of the Tartar invasions in the thirteenth century C.E. Certainly during the period of Swedish control, particularly in the Pomeranian region, there was intermarriage and mixing of cultural habits. During the early 1800s, when the Poles at first supported Napoleon's ambitions, many Polish men supported and even fought for France and later married French women. When French troops marched back and forth over Polish territory on their way to and from Russia, a number of soldiers slipped away and eventually joined Polish families, either through legal marriage or informal liaisons. There are a number of Polish names that have partly French origins. Along the eastern borders of Poland there was much intermarriage with Ukrainians.

Jewish people were known to have been in Poland by the eleventh century, and some scholars assert as early as the tenth. But they did not arrive in significant numbers until the middle of the thirteenth century, when King Casimir the Great placed Jewish communities under royal protection, valuing their skills as craftsmen (such as coin makers), merchants, and moneylenders.

By the time modern Poland was created after World War I, most Polish urban areas were a mix of people with many different backgrounds, although the majority were certainly Polish. Many urban Poles today lament the loss of this cosmopolitanism, a result of the Holocaust and the resettlement of ethnic Germans, Hungarians, and others into lands where their ancestors supposedly came from.

The nobility plays an important role in Polish folktales. Unlike the rest of Europe, in Poland this class, the *szlachta*, was very large, although usually without specific titles. The *szlachta* was composed of three classes: the so-called high nobles, who generally had huge estates and often intermarried with noble families from other parts of Europe; the middle class of nobles, who tried to emulate the higher noble class but were usually not wealthy enough to marry into it; and the petty nobility, who often owned very little land or were landless. All three classes were usually looked up to and were most often better educated than the general populace.

The male head of a noble or magnate family, if there was no official title, was referred to as Pan, his wife as Pani, and an unmarried daughter as Panna. Young males achieved the status of Pan once they reached their majority. In modern times, these words are the polite way to say mister, mistress, and miss, and have no bearing on the family's position in the *szlachta*. In the folktales in this book, these terms always refer to *szlachta* or to members of the magnate families who might or might not have been part of the *szlachta*.

CHRONOLOGY

This listing covers only the highlights of Polish history. There are of course many books that provide much more extensive information. We use B.C.E. (before the common era) and C.E. (in the common era) here, rather than B.C. and A.D.

ca. 180,000 B.C.E.	The earliest trace of human occupation, later found in the Ojcow Caves, near Krakow.
ca. 4500 B.C.E.	Linear pottery culture and arrival of Lengyel people.
ca. 2500 B.C.E.	Bronze Age and development of the Lusatian culture.
ca. 888 B.C.E.	Slavonic tribes (also known as Slavic or Slavonian) that had once been living as far to the west as what is now Germany move slightly eastward, to the other side of the Elbe River, and settle there.
ca. 550 B.C.E.	An island fortress is built near Biskupin, just south of present-day Bydgoszcz.
0–400 C.E.	Roman goods are brought to the area by traders, who return to Rome with amber and other valuable goods.
ca. 150 C.E.	Ptolemy, in his *Geography*, mentions Kalisz, the oldest Polish site with a written history.
ca. 850	Founding of the Piast Dynasty.
ca. 963–992	Reign of Mieszko I.
ca. 966	Poland becomes a Christian country through Mieszko's marriage to a Christian Czech princess. They become part of the Latin rite Christians, rather than one of the Eastern rites. This unites them more with western, rather than eastern, Europe.
ca. 991	The "Dagome judex," the oldest known Polish document, is issued by Mieszko I.
ca. 1000	The Gniezno convention takes place, during which the archbishopric of Gniezno is founded, together with the bishoprics of Krakow, Kolobrzeg, and Wroclaw.

ca. 1002–1018	Three wars with Emperor Henry II, of the Holy Roman Empire.
ca. 1025	Coronation of Boleslaw Chrobry, the first true king of Greater Poland.
ca. 1226	Konrad Mazowiecki, a princely ruler in one of the northern territories of Poland, invites the Teutonic Order to come there to help prevent attacks by Prussian tribes. The plan backfires, and the Teutonic Order itself begins to assume control of access to the Vistula River and the Baltic Sea.
1240–1241	First invasion of the Mongols (also called Tartars) under Ogotai, son of Genghis Khan. Ogotai is killed during this invasion, but his troops succeed in destroying a good part of southern Poland.
1242	Incorporation of the first Polish municipality, Wroclaw, today the capital of Lower Silesia.
1259–1260	Second invasion by the Mongols.
1287–1288	Third invasion by the Mongols.
1300–1305	Poland and Bohemia unite.
1308	Gdansk is seized by the Teutonic Order.
1364	The University of Krakow is founded by King Casimir the Great (Kazimierz Wielki), the last of the Piast Dynasty.
1370	King Casimir the Great dies, leaving a united, powerful Polish state.
1370–1385	The union of Poland and Hungary and the beginnings of the Angevin (Anjou) Dynasty.
1385	After a treaty signed in Krewa, Poland and Lithuania form a union.
1386	Wladyslaw Jagiello becomes the first king in the Jagiellonian Dynasty.
1409	The beginning of the great war with the Teutonic Order.
1410	The battle of Grunwald, in which Polish and Lithuanian forces unite to defeat the Teutonic Order, but the Order still has a hold on certain parts of Poland.
1454–1466	Continuation of the war with the Teutonic Order.
1473	The earliest printing press in Poland is set up in Krakow.
1525	The last Grand Master of the Teutonic Order, Albrecht von Hohenzollern, pays homage to the Polish King, Sigismund the Elder (Zygmunt Stary).
1569	Through a treaty known as the Lublin Union, Lithuania and the Ukraine become part of the country of Poland. That portion becomes known as the Grand Duchy of Lithuania. With that union, Poland becomes the largest country in Europe.

1543	Copernicus publishes *De Revolutionibus*.
1573	The Confederation of Warsaw signs documents guaranteeing religious tolerance. Henry Valois is elected king of Poland, and for 221 years after this, all Polish kings are elected, rather than succeeding automatically through inheritance.
1576	Stephen Batory, prince of Transylvania, is elected king of Poland.
1587	Sigismund III Waza becomes king of Poland. He moves the capital from Krakow to Warsaw.
1610	At the battle of Kluszyn, the Poles defeat the Russian czar. For almost the next fifty years, Poland enjoys peace and prosperity.
1652	The first *liberum veto*, in which every deputy in Parliament is given the right to cancel the session of Parliament. It is a symbol of freedom for the gentry.
1655–1660	Sweden invades Poland. They are stopped short at Jasna Gora Monastery in Czestochowa.
1683	Polish troops under King Jan III (John Sobieski) defeat the Turks at the Battle of Vienna, saving much of the rest of Europe from invasion.
1700–1721	The Great Northern War.
1717	The Silent Seym and the beginning of the Russian protectorate.
1764	Stanislaus Poniatowski is elected as last king of Poland.
1764–1795	The Confederation of Bar strengthens the feudal privileges of the Polish gentry. This in turn leads to a peasant uprising and the eventual intervention of Russia, setting the stage for the First Partition of Poland.
1772	The First Partition of Poland is carried out by Russia, Prussia, and Austria, who annexed one third of Polish territory. The other part remains independent.
1791	The Polish Parliament passes the May 3 Constitution and introduces major reforms, aiming to ensure Polish independence. The parliament establishes an army, brings about tax reforms, and abolishes the *liberum veto* and the elective monarchy. It also brings an end to the oligarchy of wealthy magnates.
1792	The Confederation of Targowica, formed by a few magnates, aims at eliminating the new legal measures. It takes place before the new republic is ready with an armed force to defend itself. An uneven battle with Russian troops follows, leading to the second partition of Poland.

1793	The Second Partition of Poland, undertaken by Russia and Prussia, leaves only a small independent state.
1794	The Kosciuszko Uprising, a heroic national uprising, is suppressed by czarist Russia.
1795	The Third Partition of Poland by Prussia, Austria, and Russia. Poland disappears from the political map of Europe.
1797	The Polish Legions are formed in Italy by General Dabrowski.
1807	The establishment of the Grand Duchy of Warsaw.
1815	The Congress of Vienna takes place after the final defeat of Napoleon; it hopes to restore Europe to its 1789 ruling powers but does not entirely succeed. The Kingdom of Poland and the Republic of Krakow are established.
1816	Warsaw University is established.
1830–1831	The November Insurrection, the first of many unsuccessful efforts to regain independence, begins.
1846	The Krakow Insurrection takes place.
1848	The Insurrection of Poznan occurs in response to repression by the Prussians.
1863–1864	The January Insurrection occurs as a direct result of Russia imposing compulsory military service on all young Polish men.
1876	Prussia prohibits the use of the Polish language in the area of Poland it occupies.
1914	World War I begins.
1918	World War I ends. Poland recovers independence after more than a hundred years of political nonexistence. Jozef Pilsudzki is elected as chief of state. Programs of economic and cultural development begin.
1919–1920	The Polish–Soviet War takes place.
1939–1945	World War II overwhelms all of Europe, with Poland among the first nations to be occupied when Hitler attacks on September 1, 1939, and Soviet troops attack on September 17. The Nazi occupation begins.
1939–1940	The Polish government in exile is formed.
1943	The Warsaw Uprising in the Jewish Ghetto is crushed.
1944	Another general Warsaw uprising is crushed by the Nazis.
1945	The Yalta Conference is held, at which the present borders of Poland are determined.

1946	The Polish United Workers' Party monopolizes power in the new Poland.
1956	Demonstrations against the communist system take place in Poznan.
1966	Poland observes the 1,000-year anniversary of the country's Christianity and its beginnings as a country.
1968	Student unrest occurs in Poznan, Warsaw, and Wroclaw.
1970	Workers strike and demonstrate in Gdansk; more than forty are killed and over a thousand are wounded.
1976	Workers strike and demonstrate in Radom and Ursus.
1978	Karol Wojtyla is elected Pope John Paul II.
1980	Workers strike and demonstrate in Gdansk, Szczecin, and many other cities. Solidarity is founded in Gdansk.
1981	Martial law is declared.
1989	Communist rule comes to an end with the elections of June 4, in which persons connected to Solidarity win the most seats.
1900	The first presidential elections are held and Lech Walesa is elected.
1991	The first independent parliamentary elections since World War II are held.
1995	Aleksander Kwasniewski is elected as the second president.
2000	Aleksander Kwasniewski is reelected.
2004	Poland enters the European Union
2005	Lech Kaczynski is elected as the next president.
2007	Poland becomes a member of the Schengen.

RELIGION

Since 966 the principal religion of Poland has been Roman Catholicism. Catholics currently make up 90 to 96 percent of the population. In some areas, especially in eastern Poland, Eastern Orthodox and Greek Orthodox forms of Christianity were established early on and still exist today. About 1 percent of the population is Protestant. It has been speculated that before World War II up to 5 percent of the population was Jewish. Although there are no exact figures available, it is believed that there are somewhere between 5,000 and 10,000 Jews currently living in Poland.

With the passage of laws guaranteeing freedom of religion to any group that registers officially, it is estimated that there are now some 150 religious groups of various types maintaining a presence in Poland today.

FOLK COSTUMES

The nobility, influenced by the courtly traditions of other parts of Europe (especially France), wore more elaborate dress than the common folk in the fourteenth through the fifteenth centuries. Their clothing also had always exhibited eastern influences, notably Turkish and Sarmatian. Sometime in the sixteenth century it became common for Polish nobility to insist that they were descended from the Sarmatians, a "noble warrior" class that had come from the east and settled in Poland a long time before. They believed the Sarmatians were the ancestors only of the noble class, not of the peasantry.

This preoccupation with Sarmatism influenced all forms of Polish culture from that period onward. It became important to wear extravagant clothing designed more in eastern than western style. The horse became symbolic of all that these "noble warriors" represented, so every nobleman and wealthy person tried to have a horse with elaborate trappings, as well as boots and decorated outfits to wear while riding the horse. For many nobles, the only wealth they had was in the things they wore.

The peasantry, on the other hand, as well as the freeholders, small merchants, and craft worker families, wore much simpler clothing up to the beginning of the 1800s. Those who aspired to better things attempted to imitate the nobility and began to decorate the clothing they wore on special occasions. One of the few distinctions that could indicate the part of Poland a person came from was headgear. Especially among married women, different styles of caps, hoods, and scarves were seen in many areas of Poland. Aprons also were distinctive in many areas.

With the rise of nationalism throughout Europe in the nineteenth century and the improvement of economic conditions, a more elaborate costumes developed that were worn on special occasions such as weddings and religious festivals. This was possible because cloth no longer had to be spun and woven at home, but could be purchased ready-made in the markets.

Although the components were similar (blouses, skirts, aprons, shawls, vests, knee-length trousers, jackets), the colors and decorations were different in each part of Poland. There was extraordinary variety, and each ethnic group strove to have the most distinctive combinations. The Atlas Polskich Strojow Ludowych (Atlas of Polish Peoples' Dress; see Bibliography for specific volumes in this ongoing series) illustrates how special each area's folk costume had become. The colorful patterns, stripes, embroideries, and different textures of cloth make an astounding array. In many areas folk festivals are held, during which awards are given for the finest costumes.

CALENDAR OF HOLIDAYS WITH FOLK CUSTOMS

Throughout the year, there are celebrations centered around name days, rather than birthdays. For example, if a person is named Anna, she will celebrate on July 26, and friends and family will pay her special attention, with gifts, invitations, and even poems created especially for the occasion. The same would occur on August 10 for someone named Lawrence. To celebrate these days properly in Poland, one has to have a complete calendar of saints; only a few are included in this list.

New Year's Eve   This is a favorite time for fortune telling. In many areas, it also includes groups of carolers going from house to house.

New Year's Day   Families and friends visit each other to pass on good wishes. It is also a day when silly tricks are played, similar to April Fool's Day in Great Britain and North America.

January 6   Epiphany or the Feast of the Magi or Feast of the Three Kings. This is mostly a religious celebration, although in some areas there is caroling in the costumes of the three wise men. Special cakes are sometimes baked, with symbols buried inside. This is similar to the tradition in a number of European countries.

February 2   Feast of the Purification. This honors the day on which Mary had to go to the temple to be "purified" after the birth of Jesus, as Judaic law prescribed for all women after childbirth. It is still common for candles to be decorated and taken to church to be blessed. As on Groundhog Day in the United States, in many parts of Poland people watch a bear (or some other animal) to observe what it sees when it comes out of its den, to predict either more winter or the end of winter.

February or March	Purim. On this day, Jewish families still make special foods to honor Queen Esther, who saved her people when they were in exile in Persia.
February or March	A period of merriment just before Lent begins. Traditionally, on Shrove Tuesday, the day before Ash Wednesday, in many villages groups of young men, masquerading in animal costumes, went from house to house and asked for food, drink, kisses from the young girls in the home, and dancing. There are still many parties on this day.
Between February 8 and March 7	Ash Wednesday. Beginning of Lent. Many go to church to have a cross of ashes rubbed onto their foreheads. Traditionally, strict fasting was required during the whole of Lent. This has changed somewhat, but the special foods, such as zurek (see recipe in part 2), are still served.
March 20 or 21 or the fourth Sunday in Lent	Marzanna Festival (see "Games and Seasonal Activities" in part 2).
End of March	Return of the storks to Poland.
Between March 15 and April 18	Palm or Passion Sunday or Willow Sunday. The beginning of Holy Week, this is often called Willow Sunday because in many parts of Poland where palms were not available, branches of willow were used. There are still processions, and the branches of palms, willows, or whatever plant was used are kept in special places in the home, sometimes after they are made into woven figures or symbols such as the cross.
Between Palm Sunday and Easter	Holy week. Each area of Poland seems to have its special time during this week for the coloring of eggs, the preparation of special foods, the performance of short miracle plays, and other activities. Friday is reserved for visiting various churches, which display tomb scenes. On Saturday baskets of food are taken to church to be blessed.
Between March 22 and April 25	Easter. This is the most important feast day among Christians in Poland. It is strictly a religious holiday. There are many foods associated with the day; one of the most traditional is *cwikla* (see recipe in part 2). The table is often decorated with the colored eggs and a lamb made of cake, sugar, or butter.
Easter Monday.	Dyngus. See "Games and Seasonal Activities" in part 2.

Between March and April	Passover. This Jewish feast is often called the Feast of Unleavened Bread. It celebrates the exodus. Families get together for a special meal, called a seder. During the seven or eight days of the holiday, the only bread eaten is matzoh, which is unleavened, symbolizing the haste with which the Jewish people left Egypt.
May 1	May Day. Many villages, especially in rural regions such as Kaszubia and Silesia, still put up maypoles and decorate them. This is also the beginning of a month devoted to Mary, the mother of Jesus. Many set up small shrines in their homes and keep them decorated with fresh flowers. The small wayside shrines along roads are also looked after in special ways during this month.
May or June	Shavuot. The Jewish Feast of Weeks, celebrating the reception of the Torah on Mount Sinai.
Between May 10 and June 13	Pentecost. The seventh Sunday after Easter. It is especially popular in rural Poland, where processions of persons carrying greenery and spring flowers are still common. This custom also survived until recently in Polish American rural areas. In some parts of Poland, farm animals such as cows or horses are decorated with flowers or wreaths, and races are held to see who has the fastest animals in the area.
Between May 21 and June 24	Corpus Christi. This feast, falling eleven days after Pentecost, is celebrated with the construction of small altars or wreaths in front of many homes and buildings. Masses are often held on outdoor altars, rather than inside churches. Many farmers use it as an occasion to have seeds blessed.
June 23	Eve of Saint John's Day. This day retains many elements of pre-Christian customs. Often herbs are gathered. In the evening bonfires are lit, and people sing and dance around them. (See "The Flower of the Fern" in part 5.)
July 13	Saint Margaret's Day. This was the day rutabagas were planted, so as to have them ready for a late harvest. In the Kaszubian region, on the Sunday after this or the first Sunday after July 16, the first wheat was cut and made into a special loaf of bread.
August through September	Harvest festivals. These occurred at different times in different parts of Poland, and lasted through Septem-

ber. (See "Wianki" in "Games and Seasonal Activities" in part 2.)

August 15	Assumption of Our Lady. Another favorite day for the gathering of herbs, which were then taken to church to be blessed.
September	The preferred month for weddings.
September or October	Rosh Hashanah. The Jewish holy day that begins the New Year. Many Jewish families eat apples dipped in honey and wish each other a "sweet year."
September or October	Yom Kippur. This falls ten days after Rosh Hashanah and is the holiest day in the Jewish calendar. It is also called the Day of Atonement, and is a day of fasting, prayer, and asking for forgiveness.
November 1	All Saints' Day. This was mainly used as a preparation for the next day. Bread was baked in great quantities, for giving to the poor.
November 2	All Souls' Day. A day of prayer for relatives and friends who have died, and also a time for sharing with the poor.
November 11	Saint Martin's Day. This French saint is greatly revered in Poland. Legend says he was about to be elected pope and did not want this position, so he hid in a big flock of geese. Therefore, it is traditional to serve roast goose on this day.
Between November 27 and December 3	First Sunday of Advent. In churches and homes, a candelabra with seven candles, called *roraty*, is lit. *Roraty* comes from the Latin in Isaiah 45, verse 8: "*Rorate coeli …*" (Drop down dew, ye heavens, from above, and let the clouds rain justice; let the earth be opened and bud forth a Savior.) The seven candles symbolize the social classes in Poland, from peasant to king.
December 4	Saint Barbara's Day. On this day, families still put a branch of cherry or another tree into a jar of water, and force it to bloom by Christmas.
December 6	Saint Nicholas's Day. This is celebrated in some parts of Poland on the evening before, on this day, or even on the Sunday closest to the day. Men dress up like bishops (*not* like Santa Claus) and go from house to house, or school to school, asking children if they have

Traditional costume of Koleda during post-Christmas time, 1958. Photo courtesy of the Ethnographical Museum of Warsaw. Photo by Stefan Deptuszewski.

been good. The children are often rewarded with *pierniki* (see "Food" in part 2).

December 15 through Epiphany Various groups perform *szopka* plays, either in the streets or in theaters and other indoor locations. *Szopka* means crib, and the plays performed in the streets are accompanied by a handmade stand supporting either a crib scene or a church scene with figures of Mary, Joseph, the baby Jesus, and other characters in the play, such as Herod, the shepherds, or the Three Kings. The plays are similar to medieval mystery plays, and many of the texts are centuries old.

December 22 Saint Thomas's Day. Children take fir branches from home to home, wishing everyone, "Happy Saint Thomas Day, and may no one be sick or blind in this home." The branch is used to touch all the animals in the house or barn, and it is then hung in a safe place. The children are rewarded with sweets or coins of small value.

December 24 Christmas Eve. Many preparations begin early in the day. The top of a fir or spruce tree is selected and hung from a central point in the ceiling, upside down, so the tip is facing downward. It is then decorated with fake spiders and webs, paper chains, ornaments made from wheat straw, and other handmade items. A round orna-ment, symbolizing the earth, is hung at the very bottom tip. Before the meal is served that evening, a wafer of unleavened bread, called *oplatek*, is shared among all those present. From oldest to youngest, they break off a small piece of the wafer, hand it to the next in line, and wish her or him a long and happy life. The meal is meatless, and sometimes consists of eleven or twelve foods to symbolize the apostles. Just a taste or slice of something suffices. The table often has straw spread under the cloth, a reminder of the stable where Jesus was born. Later in the evening, groups of children or young adults go caroling, often carrying a star on a pole. These are called *gwiazdory, gwiazdki,* or various dialect names meaning "star." In Kaszubia they are called *gvjostki,* and are more often composed of young men dressed in animal costumes. (See the chapters in Anne Pellowski's books, *First Farm in the Valley* and *Winding Valley Farm,* for a description of how this custom was transposed to North America.) In other parts of Poland, these masked young men are called *torun.* Many families attend midnight mass.

Traditional costume of Koleda during post-Christmas time, with the performance of Herod's tempta-tion by the devil and the cutting of the head of Herod, 1960, Gostwice in Nowosadeckie area. Photo courtesy of the Ethnographical Museum of Warsaw. Photo by Bohdan Czarnecki, 1960.

December 25	Christmas. This is strictly a family day, celebrated with good food and relaxing at home. Little or no visiting is done.
December 26	Saint Stephen's Day. This is the day for visiting. Families often take food to share with others. Similar to "first footing" in parts of Great Britain, traditionally the first child visitor to cross the doorway of a home was given a treat.
December or January	Hanukkah. On this joyous Jewish festival of eight days, the evening always opens with the lighting of one candle. The menorah, or special candelabra, often has a ninth candle that is used to light the others. There is often exchanging of gifts, singing of songs, and playing games with the dreidel.

Traditional costume of Koleda during post-Christmas time, in Jaworzynka, 1981.
Photo courtesy of the Ethnographical Museum of Warsaw. Photo by Lubomir Kosiñski.

STORYTELLING IN POLAND

Poland has a long storytelling tradition, dating back to pre-Christian times. The arrival of Christianity in Poland in 966 was accompanied by efforts to destroy all polytheistic beliefs and early mythology. Not much is known about these pre-Christian oral traditions. A few remnants survive, such as the names and characteristics of some of the early gods: Perkun, Swiatowid, and others.

From medieval documents it is possible to ascertain that various forms of storytelling flourished all over Poland. Bards were popular for their recitations of epic poetry, using chant mixed with song. The bards traveled from town to town or were retained as servants by noble households, or in some cases by innkeepers.

Traveling beggars called *dziad* (meaning grandfather) performed chanted stories called *piesnie dziadowskie*. These were religious legends or dramatic stories of real life, centered around such enthralling events as unrequited love resulting in suicide, murder, robbery, and the like. These beggar storytellers played an instrument called *lira korbowa* and usually performed at markets or outside churches on festival days, catching the people's attention as they exited from church. The last singer storytellers of this type performed in Czestochowa several decades ago.

Also important in the Polish storytelling tradition were village storytellers, who learned stories from their ancestors and passed them on orally. Such storytelling was done after harvest time, or on evenings of feast days when the villagers had gathered together and wanted some entertainment. This tradition barely survived into the latter part of the twentieth century.

However, although they rarely perform for entire villages, there are still people who retain a font of stories heard in childhood. During two months of field work in Mazovia in 2006, Michał Malinowski collected more than 200 parts of tales or entire stories. These varied from animal stories, to local and religious legends, to humorous tales and ghost stories. Most were told not as imaginary tales of the past, but as events that had happened to someone whom the teller knew. The informants, whose average age was eighty, remembered that during their childhoods telling tales and singing songs was a regular routine. They would often say they did not remember the stories well, but would say: "If only you could have heard so-and-so, now he/she was a real storyteller." Most often, the person referred to was deceased.

Awareness of their heritage of an oral tradition influenced many writers (one can call them folklorists only in a very loose sense) to begin collecting folk stories and publishing them. This occurred so soon after the publication of the Grimm brothers' collection that it was likely influenced by their work.

The first collector of folktales and folk songs in Poland was Zorian Dolega Chodakowski, pseudonym of the writer Adam Czarnocki. He wrote and published in 1818 a very influential pamphlet about pre-Christian times in Poland (see Bibliography). Unfortunately it contains only brief mentions of early gods and myths. The folktales he collected were never published, although one small book of folk songs he collected did appear in print.

In 1837 the first extensive collection of tales made its appearance. It was written by Kazimierz Wojcicki, and at least some of the tales in that collection are still in print. Another early collector was Jozef Lompa, who published the tales he encountered in Silesia, first in periodicals, and finally in a book. Roman Zmorski found most of the tales he published in his 1852 collection in Mazovia. Other writers, such as Lucjan Sieminski, A. J. Glinski, Jozef I. Kraszewski, Sadok Baracz, and Adolf Dygasinski, collected tales from various parts of Poland during the nineteenth century, but often rewrote the tales in literary style.

The most impressive ethnographic work was done by Oskar Kolberg. He began collecting folk songs, folktales, proverbs, folk rituals, and rhymes sometime before 1848 and continued until his death in 1890. The complete collection of his work has reached eighty-seven volumes, and some volumes are still being edited. It is probably only because Polish is such a difficult language for non-Poles to learn that his reputation in the international field of folklore is so little known. There is no other country in which the folk language and lore from that period has been so thoroughly documented.

Most traditional storytellers of the nineteenth century remain anonymous, but there is one in Poland who is well known by name. Jan Krzeptowski, called Sabala (1809–1893), was discovered in the Tatra mountains by some intellectuals, who regularly hiked there with guides. While acting as one of these guides, Sabala told stories in such a vivid way that he was called "the Homer of the Tatras." He often accompanied his telling by playing his fiddle. He had a significant influence on Sienkiewicz and other writers. His tales, songs, and a biography were published by A. Stopka in 1897.

To this day, storytelling has been kept alive in the Tatra Mountain region. Every year, in the town of Bukowina Tatrzanska, near Zakopane, there is a storytelling festival, named in honor of Sabala. It brings together traditional storytellers, musicians, and folk artists from all over Poland, as well as other countries.

Folk storytelling in Poland has experienced a revival in recent years. In 2002 the Storyteller Museum opened in Konstancin-Jeziorna, near Warsaw. It was founded by Michał Malinowski, who is its director. The primary goals of the museum are to preserve and promote the oral heritage of Poland and of the world, as well as to find a means of using the collective wisdom of the ages in modern contexts. Another goal is to present the entire context of oral narration, including such things as body movement and gesture, dance, ritual aspects, costumes, body painting, and musical accompaniment, rather than only recording texts on audiotape, which often separates them from important parts of the narration process. The museum presents live performances and also hopes to record some in such a way that all aspects of the performance come through. In addition to the performances at the museum itself, the director organizes storytelling events and workshops in venues all over Poland.

Sabała, the most famous Polish storyteller. Photo courtesy of The
Tatra Museum in Zakopane. Photo by Benedykt Tyszkiewicz.

In 2004 the museum organized a Storytelling Festival in the French Language. Storytellers from France, Switzerland, Belgium, Canada, and French-speaking African countries were brought together for performances and discussions. Every year since that time, a festival called Teznia Marzen has combined traditional storytelling with the contemporary forms of storytelling now found internationally. A Jewish Storytelling Festival was held in 2006. From among the attendees at these festivals, and at various workshops, the Polish Storytelling Association, Imagana, has been formed.

There are a few other Polish groups and individuals actively pursuing the art: Grupa Studnia O, a group of seven individual tellers; the Jewish storytelling group organized by Witold Dabrowski in Lublin under the auspices of the Association Brama Grodzka; and Jacek Halas, storytelling in his traveling tent.

Contemporary storytelling in Poland is not yet as popular as it is in North American countries, but it is alive and growing.

FOLK ARTS AND MUSIC

A number of the folk arts in Poland are directly tied into storytelling because of their content. Characters and scenes from folklore were often the subjects of paper cuts (*wycinanki*), tapestries, reverse paintings on glass, and similar folk art expressions.

However, the closest ties are found in music. As noted in the previous chapter, it was common for bards and itinerant storytellers to accompany themselves on musical instruments, or to use chant as their way of putting a story across to the audience. There is evidence that Polish knights of the fifteenth century were very accomplished in performing chants that recounted religious tales or heroic deeds.

The traditional Polish wedding ceremony had many story songs attached to it. It lasted at least two days, and each step had a corresponding song. Kolberg (see Bibliography) describes many of the ceremonies in great detail; later ethnographers interpreted them as social drama of the highest quality.

The *dziad*, mentioned in the previous chapter, were not the only itinerant tellers in the nineteenth century. Some were also influenced by the *bankelsanger* tradition from other parts of Europe. These men (almost exclusively) carried large picture sheets on which were depicted scenes of riveting stories from real life, such as being saved from a fire, almost getting run over by one of the trains that started appearing in the latter part of the century, or being deceived by a lover. The men passed from market to market, hung up their colorful picture sheets, stood on a bench, and used pointers to show the relevant scenes from the story, reciting their tales in a kind of chant. This kind of storytelling was used by Kaszubians to keep their language alive at a time when the Prussian government was attempting to enforce a policy of complete Germanization. In the Kartuzy Kaszubian Museum are a few examples of such sheets, and the museum docents there often interpret them in performance. They usually accompany themselves on an instrument known as "the devil's violin." It stands on the floor and has only one string.

The great storyteller Sabala also used a kind of violin or fiddle to accompany his telling. It was the most common instrument for accompanying tales, but by no means the only one. The bagpipes were (and are) found in many parts of Poland. There were three main types, the *dudy*, *koziol*, and *gajdy*; all were handmade. Besides often being used for dancing, they were also used in interludes between storytelling.

PART 2

Food, Games, Riddles, and Nursery Rhymes

FOOD

The following recipes represent only a small segment of the special foods prepared by Polish people for everyday or special occasions. For many more recipes and food facts, consult the books cited in the list at the end of this chapter.

Recipes

Zocerka (Milk and Egg Dumpling Porridge)

This Kaszubian recipe has been passed down in the Pellowski family since the late 1850s, when they first arrived in the United States. It was served at any meal, depending on the season. It is also a comfort food, and was often served when a person was sick. It requires two persons to achieve the right consistency for the dumplings. Before assembling the dough, make sure you have a large pot of water, at least 2½ quarts, just at the point of boiling.

Ingredients:

2 cups flour, sifted

1 tsp salt

1 large egg

¼ cup milk, plus 1 tbsp

1½ cups milk

additional salt, and freshly ground pepper, to taste; other seasoning if desired, such as dried dill, cinnamon, nutmeg, or cardamom

Directions:

1. Combine flour and 1 tsp salt in a large bowl. Make a well (an indentation) in the center.

2. Beat the egg well with the ¼ cup milk and pour into the well. With a fork, briskly mix it into the flour, until just moistened. If the mixture is too dry, add the 1 tbsp milk.

3. Over the pot of boiling water, take a handful of the dough between both hands and rub together, allowing very small pieces to drop into the water while the second person constantly stirs it with a slotted spoon. Repeat until the dough is all in the boiling water. (If the pieces are larger than a lima bean, the person stirring the water should use the edge of the spoon to cut them into smaller pieces by pressing them against the side of the pot.)

4. Simmer for 3 to 4 minutes, stirring about three times per minute. Test one of the larger pieces to see if it is cooked through. When the pieces are cooked, empty the pot into a large sieve or colander, draining off most of the water. (It is not necessary to wait until all of the water is drained off.) Quickly return the dumplings to the pot. Add enough of the 1½ cups milk to make a loose porridge, about the consistency of cooked oatmeal. Add salt and freshly ground pepper to taste, as well as other seasonings if desired.

Serves 4.

Krupnik (Barley Soup)

Ingredients:

1 tbsp butter or oil
1 large onion, chopped fine
1 cup pearl barley
8 cups water
4 large carrots, sliced
2 celery stalks, sliced
1 large rutabaga, cut into cubes (optional)
8 oz sliced mushrooms
2 tbsp dried dill
salt and pepper to taste
3 tbsp chopped fresh parsley

Directions:

1. In a large saucepan, sauté onions in butter or oil for about 3 minutes.

2. Add pearl barley and stir until coated with oil.

3. Add water and bring to a boil. Boil gently for 15 minutes.

4. Add potatoes, carrots, celery, and rutabaga. Simmer until barley and vegetables are tender, about 15 minutes.

5. Add mushrooms and dill and simmer a few more minutes.

6. Add salt and pepper to taste, turn off heat, and serve with fresh parsley sprinkled over each portion.

Serves 10–12.

Zurek (Sour Rye Soup)

One must have a taste for sour things to enjoy this. It is an acquired taste. Most Poles would insist on having this at least once during Advent and Lent. In some places in Poland it is made with oatmeal or with a mixture of oatmeal and rye. For Easter morning breakfast, it is traditional to have a bowl of it with Polish sausage.

Ingredients:

For the base (or zur*):*

> 1 cup boiling water
>
> 1 cup rye flour, preferably stone ground
>
> ½ to 1 cup lukewarm water

For the soup:

> 1 small onion, chopped fine
>
> 8 oz sliced mushrooms
>
> 1 tbsp for sauteing onion and mushrooms
>
> 4 cups vegetable stock
>
> 6 medium or 4 large potatoes, cut into cubes
>
> 2 cups base (or *zur*)
>
> 1 clove garlic, crushed
>
> salt and pepper to taste

Directions:

To make the base (or zur*):*

1. In a large bowl, pour the boiling water over the rye flour and stir to form a thin dough, the consistency of pancake batter. Let cool briefly, then, add the lukewarm water. Stir well.

2. Pour into a quart-size glass jar, fasten a piece of cheesecloth over the mouth of the jar with a rubber band, and leave in a warm place for at least 2 days.

To make the soup:

1. In a large saucepan, sauté onions and mushrooms in butter for a few minutes.

2. Add stock and bring to a boil.

3. Add potatoes and 2 cups zur; boil gently until potatoes are soft.

4. Add crushed garlic, salt, and pepper.

Serves 6–8.

Sauerkraut with Yellow Peas

This is one of the twelve traditional dishes served on Christmas Eve. It used to be the custom to have twelve foods in honor of the twelve apostles. This custom has almost died out, but setting an extra place for an unknown guest who might wander in or be asked to join is still very much honored. (The dessert at this meal invariably includes poppy seed and honey, in the belief this will provide a sweet sleep to mimic the sleep of the baby Jesus.)

Ingredients:

1 cup dried yellow peas (found in specialty stores)

3 small bay leaves

1½ tsp salt

20 tiny white potatoes, cooked (may be canned)

1 tsp freshly ground black pepper

2 lbs sauerkraut

8 oz chopped mushrooms, cooked in butter or oil (optional)

8 slices crisp cooked bacon, crumbled (optional)

Directions:

1. Cover peas with cold water and let stand overnight.

2. Drain peas and place in 4-quart pot. Cover with fresh cold water. Add bay leaves and salt. Bring to a boil, then simmer until peas are almost tender.

3. Remove bay leaves. Add sauerkraut and cook on medium until peas are completely tender.

4. Add potatoes, pepper, and sauerkraut. Heat until thoroughly hot.

5. Stir in mushrooms and bacon if desired.

Serves 8–10.

Cwikla (Red Beets with Horseradish)

This relish is almost always included in the Easter meal. The red symbolizes blood and the sharpness, the gall Jesus was forced to taste.

Ingredients:

2 tsp sugar

4 cups chopped, cooked beets (canned may be used)

3–5 tbsp prepared horseradish

Directions:

1. In a glass dish, stir sugar into beets.

2. Add 2 tbsp horseradish and taste. Keep adding until you achieve a very sharp taste, but not so sharp you cannot enjoy it.

3. Stir well. Place in a covered glass quart jar and refrigerate for 2 to 3 days before using.

Serves up to 12 as a side relish.

Pierogi

These filled dumplings come in so many varieties it would take many pages to list them all. Provided here are the recipes for a few of the best-known fillings and the dough. Prepare your filling(s) before you prepare the dough, allowing enough time for them to cool and be handled easily. Also, have a large pot of water, almost boiling, ready before you begin rolling out the dough.

Cabbage or sauerkraut and mushroom filling

Ingredients:

1 cup sauerkraut or cabbage, cooked and chopped into very small pieces, either by hand or in a food processor.

2 tbsp finely chopped onion

1 tbsp oil or butter

4 oz mushrooms, sliced

1 hard-boiled egg, chopped fine

salt and pepper

Directions:

1. If using sauerkraut, drain well. If using cabbage, cook until tender, drain well, and set aside.

2. Sauté onion in butter or oil for 5 minutes.

3. Add mushrooms and sauté for 3–5 minutes, until they give off liquid.

4. Strain onion and mushroom mixture so no liquid is left.

5. Place in a bowl and add cabbage or sauerkraut (with all water pressed out) and chopped egg. Add salt and pepper to taste.

Will fill 24–30 pierogi.

Cheese filling

Ingredients:

1½ cups cottage cheese

1 egg

salt and pepper

Directions:

1. Drain cottage cheese well by letting it stand in a sieve over a bowl, for several hours or placing it in cheesecloth and gently squeezing until all liquid is squeezed out.

2. Beat egg well and add to drained cottage cheese.

3. Add salt and pepper to taste.

Will fill 24–30 pierogi.

Meat filling

Ingredients:

1 onion, chopped fine

1 tbsp butter or oil

1 cup leftover cooked meat, chopped very fine by hand or in a food processor

Directions:

1. Fry onion in oil until golden.

2. Turn off heat and stir in meat.

Will fill 24 pierogi.

Potato filling

Ingredients:

1 onion, chopped very fine

1 tbsp butter or oil

1 cup mashed potatoes (made without milk or egg; do not use packaged type)

½ cup dry farmer's cheese, crumbled

salt and pepper to taste

Directions:

1. Fry onion in butter or oil and add to mashed potatoes.

2. Add crumbled farmer's cheese and mix well.

3. Add salt and pepper.

Will fill 24–30 pierogi.

Fruit filling

Ingredients:

¼ cup sugar

2 tbsp quick-cooking tapioca

1½ cups fresh or frozen fruit, chopped fine and drained well (save juice) or

1½ cups dried fruit, simmered gently in sugar water until soft, then chopped fine

Directions:

1. Combine sugar and tapioca.

2. Add to fruit and fold in well.

3. Let stand at least 15 minutes before putting into pierogi pockets.

Will fill 24–30 pierogi.

Pierogi Dough

There are many variations of this dough. Some use cottage cheese; others use sour cream. Some do not use egg; some use milk. Some specialty stores sell pierogi wraps already prepared, similar to Chinese won ton wraps. (In one cookbook it was recommended that one substitute the latter; the results would be similar.) This is one of the simpler recipes and will make about 24 to 30 pierogi, depending on the size. They can be cut into either squares or circles.

Ingredients:

3 cups flour

1 tsp salt

1 medium egg

½ cup plus 1–2 tbsp water

extra flour for rolling out dough

Directions:

1. As mentioned above, have water in a large pot almost at boiling point.

2. Combine flour and salt.

3. Beat egg and water together and pour ⅔ of it into flour. Mix.

4. Knead lightly. Add just enough water to make a dough that is not too sticky and can be rolled out easily.

5. Place ⅓ of dough on floured board. Keep remainder covered with damp paper towel.

6. Roll out dough and cut into 3–4-inch circles or squares.

7. Using fingertip or small brush, wet ½ of edges of circles or squares with water.

8. Put 1 or 2 tsp of filling in center of each. Fold over into half circles or triangles. Press down edges with fork.

9. Place pierogi on large cookie sheet without overlapping and cover with lightly dampened towel until ready to drop into boiling water.

10. Repeat with rest of dough.

11. Gently drop 8 to 10 pierogi into boiling water, maintaining a gently rolling boil They will sink to the bottom. When they come to the top, simmer for 3–4 more minutes and then remove with a slotted spoon. Drain. Repeat until all pierogi are cooked.

Serve warm pierogi immediately, topped with crumbled bacon, sour cream, or caramelized onions. Fruit pierogi are usually topped with a sprinkling of powdered sugar or a tablespoon of the juice left over from draining the fruit. Some prefer to let meat, potato, or cheese pierogi cool and then fry them in a little bacon fat.

Bigos (Hunter's Stew)

This is one of Poland's national dishes, and it has at least as many versions as there are cities in Poland. The earliest mention of it dates to about 1800. The most famous description occurs in the epic poem *Pan Tadeusz* (1834), by Adam Mickiewicz. To make it more closely resemble the earliest type, use at least some game, such as venison. The greater variety of meat used, the better. It is often made one or two days in advance, refrigerated, then reheated.

Ingredients:

2 oz dried wild mushrooms or 1 lb sliced fresh mushrooms

½ lb bacon

1 large onion, chopped fine

2–3 lbs. leftover cooked meat such as beef, pork, ham, sausage, chicken, turkey, or venison, OR

    ½ lb pork loin cut into small pieces

    ¼ lb ham cut into chunks

    ½ lb beef stew chunks

    ½ lb venison, wild turkey, pheasant, or similar game, cut into pieces

2 lbs sauerkraut, with juice

½ lb Polish sausage (preferably smoked links, rather than the modern rings of kielbasa)

1 large bay leaf

15 peppercorns

12 pitted prunes (optional)

Directions:

1. If using dried mushrooms, wash them, then simmer in 1 cup water for about 10 minutes and drain, saving the water. When cool, slice and set aside.

2. Fry bacon until very crisp and set aside.

3. Pour off half the bacon grease from pan and stir the onions into the remaining fat. Sauté until light golden.

4. Transfer onions to a large, heavy pot. You will need at least a 4-quart pot with a cover. (This can be a large crock pot.)

5. Brown meat in same pan used for cooking onions.

6. Transfer meat to the large pot, add sauerkraut, and simmer slowly for 2 hours.

7. Add mushrooms (and juice if using dried mushrooms), sausage, bay leaf, and peppercorns.

8. Simmer slowly, covered, for at least 2 more hours. (If using cooked meats, simmer only a total of 2 hours, putting everything into the pot at the same time, except the prunes.)

9. Taste one of the pieces of meat to see if tender and cooked through. Sprinkle bacon and prunes into the pot and stir in.

10. Simmer for 10 more minutes. Add more salt if necessary.

11. Take pot off heat, let cool, and refrigerate overnight or up to 48 hours.

12. Reheat and serve with boiled potatoes and rye bread.

Serves 12.

Fried Buckwheat Slices

Buckwheat is one of the most-used grains in traditional Polish cooking. It is very high in nutrients. It is found in most large grocery stores in whole grain or cracked grain versions. If simply cooked in water and lightly seasoned, it is often referred to as kasha.

Most older Polish cookbooks describe a method of cooking it and later slicing and frying it. This came to be known as *kiszka* among many North American Poles, although *kiszka* usually refers to a buckwheat and pork smoked sausage, often of the blood sausage type. A well-known American polka is called "Who Stole the Kiszka?"

Ingredients:

4 cups water

1 tsp salt

2 cups cracked buckwheat groats

1 large egg

1 large potato, boiled and mashed, allowed to cool until lukewarm

½ lb bacon, fried crisply and crumbled, or ½ lb pork lardons, fried until crisp (optional)

Directions:

1. In a large pot, boil water and add salt and buckwheat groats.

2. Cook over medium heat, stirring constantly. Continue cooking and stirring until it is very difficult to stir the mass. Remove from heat.

3. Beat egg until frothy and add to lukewarm mashed potato.

4. Add a spoonful of the hot groats to the egg mixture and stir in to prevent egg from curdling. Add another spoonful and again stir in.

5. Add the egg mixture to the large pot, then add the bacon or lardon crisps, and mix in well. Add salt if needed and several turns of freshly ground pepper.

6. Oil two small or one large loaf pan and pat the buckwheat mixture into them/it. Press down firmly with a spatula. Place waxed paper or plastic wrap directly on top of the buckwheat mixture. Put a heavy jar or can on top of the wrap and refrigerate overnight.

7. Turn pan over onto a board. The buckwheat should come out easily.

8. Slice in ½-inch-thick slices and fry (in butter, oil, or bacon fat) on both sides until very crisp.

Serves 6–8.

Dried Fruit Compote

This is a favorite dish at Christmas and New Year's dinners. It can be a combination of dried fruits.

Ingredients:

2 lbs mixed dried fruit such as pitted prunes, apples, apricots, figs, peaches, pears, raisins, cranberries, etc.; cut into bite-sized pieces if the dried segments are large

8–10 cups water

½ cup honey

4 tbsp fresh lemon juice

1 tbsp grated lemon rind

Directions:

1. In a glass bowl or similar container, generously cover fruit with water and soak for 24 hours in refrigerator.

2. Drain water from fruit into a heavy saucepan.

3. Add honey and bring to a simmer.

4. Add lemon juice and zest and pour over fruit in original glass bowl.

5. Cover with plastic wrap and refrigerate at least 4 hours.

Serves 10–12.

Piernik (Honey Cake)

This type of cake, baked in a cake pan and cut into squares, or baked on cookie sheets and decorated with colored icing, has been a favorite for many centuries. The most famous versions come from the city of Torun. This recipe is the layer cake version, but the same dough can be rolled out and cut into cookies. Chill the dough for a few hours before rolling it out.

Ingredients:

4 tbsp sugar

¼ cup boiling water

2 cups (16 oz) honey

10 tbsp butter

2 eggs

1½ tsp baking soda

½ tsp salt

1 tsp cinnamon

½ tsp cloves

½ tsp ginger

½ tsp cardamom

5 cups sifted flour

Icing:

3 tbsp butter

2 cups powdered sugar

1 to 2 tbsp milk or cream

⅓ cup cocoa (optional)

Directions:

1. Heat 4 tbsp sugar in heavy pan with high sides, stirring until brown.
2. Slowly add boiling water (it is likely to bubble up).
3. Continue stirring, adding honey and butter and heat until melted. Remove from heat and let cool until lukewarm.
4. Beat eggs, then add 1 tbsp of lukewarm mixture and mix well. Then add another tbsp.
5. Combine eggs with rest of lukewarm honey mixture.
6. Add soda, salt, and spices to sifted flour and mix well.
7. Add flour and spice mixture to honey/butter/sugar/egg mixture. Stir well and knead lightly. Dough should be fairly stiff.
8. Knead into a ball, place in a buttered dish, cover tightly, and let sit in refrigerator for up to a week. If baking immediately, place in refrigerator until completely cool.
9. When ready to bake, grease two small cookie sheets or shallow rectangular cake pans. Divide dough in half and spread it onto/into cookie sheets or pans, leaving at least 1 inch space between the dough and the edge of the pan all around.
10. Preheat oven to 350°F. Bake for 12–15 minutes. Test with toothpick to see if done. Let cool on racks.
11. When cool, spread a filling of jam (plum, strawberry, raspberry, etc.) on one layer and place second layer on top. If preferred, spread a filling of one cup of chopped walnuts combined with ¼ cup caramelized sugar.
12. Cover with waxed paper and put a book on top. Let sit for 2 hours.
13. Take off book and waxed paper and cover cake with icing.

To make icing:

1. Melt butter in a double boiler or in a bowl set over a saucepan of boiling water.
2. Add powdered sugar and stir well. Add milk or cream, alternating with cocoa if desired. Add only enough liquid to make a smooth icing. Stir constantly and do not allow to get near boiling point.
3. Turn off heat and let sit for about 10 minutes.
4. Spread over honey cake. Cut into squares and serve.

Serves 12–14.

Polish Cookbooks in English

Baruch, Michael J. *The New Polish Cuisine.* New York: LBCM Publishing, 2002.

Cantrell, Rose. *Polish Cooking.* New York: Weathervane Books, 1978.

Czerny, Zofia. *Polish Cookbook.* Warsaw: Panstwowe Wydawnictwo Ekonomiczne, 1975.

Debski, Henryk. *A Contemporary Polish Cookbook.* Warsaw: Interpress Publishers, 1990.

Dembinska, Maria. *Food and Drink in Medieval Poland: Rediscovering a Cuisine of the Past.* Translated by Magdalena Thomas. Revised and adapted by William Woys Weaver. Philadelphia: University of Pennsylvania Press, 1999.

Ferguson, Judith. *Step by Step Polish Cooking.* Ann Arbor, MI: Popular Culture Ink, 1989.

The Fraternal Gourmet. Park Ridge, IL: Polish Women's Alliance of America, 1986.

Gorgey, Maria de. *A Treasury of Polish Cuisine: Traditional Recipes in Polish and English.* New York: Hippocrene Books, 1999.

Heberle, Marianna Olszewska. *Polish Cookery.* New York: HP Books, 1985.

Jones, Bridget. *Recipes from a Polish Kitchen.* New York: Smithmark Publishers, 1990.

Knab, Sophie Hodorowicz. *The Polish Country Kitchen Cookbook.* Illustrated by Elliott Hutten. New York: Hippocrene Books, 2002.

Koszyca, Czes. *Polish Cooking in South Australia.* Adelaide: Polish Women's Association, 1996.

Kowalska, Lili. *Cooking the Polish Way.* London: Spring Books, 1964.

Lemnis, Maria, and Henryk Vitry. *Old Polish Traditions in the Kitchen and at the Table.* New York: Hippocrene, 1996.

Lussiana, Bernard, and Mary Picinska. *Poland's Gourmet Cuisine.* Photos by Jaroslaw Madejski. New York: Hippocrene Books, 1999.

Nowakowski, Jacek. *Pleasing Polish Recipes.* Iowa City, IA: Penfield Press, 1989.

Nowakowski, Jacek, and Marlene Perrin. *Polish Touches: Recipes and Traditions.* Iowa City, IA: Penfield Press, 1996.

Peterson, Joan, and David Peterson. *Eat Smart in Poland: How to Decipher the Menu, Know the Market Foods and Embark on a Tasting Adventure.* Illustrated by Susie V. Medaris. Madison, WI: Gingko Press, 2000.

Pininska, Mary. *A Little Polish Cookbook.* Denton, TX: Appletree Press, 1992.

Polish Cookbook. Illustrated by Joanna Adamska-Koperska. Melrose Park, IL: Culinary Arts Institute, 1978. (Later editions edited by Sherrill Corley.)

Rysia. *Old Warsaw Cook Book.* New York: Roy Publishers, 1958.

Sawka, Hanka, and Hanna Maria Sawka. *At Hanka's Table.* New York: Lake Isle Press, 2004.

Sokolowski, Marie, and Irene Jasinski. *Treasured Polish Recipes for Americans.* Minneapolis, MN: Polanie, 1954.

Strybel, Robert, and Maria Strybel. *Polish Heritage Cookery.* 2d ed. Photos by Zbigniew Pomaski and Andrzej Karczewski. New York: Hippocrene Books, 1997.

Walczak, Malgorzata, and Michael Jacobs. *Polish Cooking.* Warsaw: Exlibris, 1998.

West, Karen. *The Best of Polish Cooking; Recipes for Entertaining and Special Occasions.* New York: Hippocrene Books, 1983.

Wirkowski, Eugeniusz. *Cooking the Polish-Jewish Way.* Warsaw: Interpress, 1988.

Zamojska-Hutchins, Danuta. *Cooking the Polish Way.* Photos by Robert L. and Diane Wolfe. Minneapolis, MN: Lerner, 1984.

Zeranska, Alina. *The Art of Polish Cooking.* Garden City, New York: Doubleday, 1968.

GAMES AND SEASONAL ACTIVITIES

Games

Berek (Tag) and Chowanego (Hide and Seek)

Both of these games are played in a manner similar to the way they are played in North America. If played at night, a flashlight is often used.

Ciuciubabka (Blindman's Buff or Bluff)

This is played with a slight difference in Poland.

Directions:

1. The person chosen to be "It" and wear the blindfold often has his or her hands tied behind the back.

2. As all the others in the game approach "It" in turn, each calls out a word or touches "It" somewhere on the upper body. She or he must recognize the one touching her or him by recognizing the voice, the manner of walking, or even the special smell each person has.

3. Once a person has been identified correctly, that person becomes "It."

Dogs and Rabbits

This is a variant of hide and seek. It is also called "Falcons and Pigeons." Teamwork is very important because the "dogs" must agree where best to look for and surround a "rabbit" and chase her or him toward the hunter.

Directions:

1. Two teams are selected. One team consists of rabbits. A second team, no more than half the number of rabbits, is made up of dogs.

2. One person is selected to be the hunter. The hunter remains standing at home base.

3. The "rabbits" go and hide.

4. The "dogs" then look for them, but don't try to catch them. Instead, they try to chase them in the direction of the hunter.

5. When the hunter touches a "rabbit," he or she is out of the game.

Old Albert

This has many different names, depending on the part of Poland in which it is played. It is a circle game.

Directions:

1. One child is selected to stand in the middle of the circle. That child acts out a type of activity or work.

2. Each person in the circle must imitate the action.

3. If the child in the middle catches someone in the circle who is not repeating the action correctly, she or he points to that person, who must take a turn in the middle of the circle and act out a different activity or work.

Pigpen and Swineherd

This is particularly suited to playing at the beach or along a sandy lake shore.

Directions:

1. One player is selected to start as the "swineherd." That player holds the ball (the "pig") and a stick or bat.

2.	A hole large enough to hold the size of ball being played with is dug in a central spot. In a circle around it a series of smaller holes are dug, one for each player except the "swineherd."

3.	Each of the players has a stick or bat, which they stand up in the small holes, one per hole.

4.	The "swineherd" tries to move the ball with his stick so as to get it into the center hole.

5.	The other players attempt to prevent this by holding out their sticks and sending the "pig" back to the "swineherd."

6.	If the "swineherd" catches one of the players with her or his stick out of the hole and the "swineherd" manages to stand his or her stick in that hole, the player who got caught with the stick out of the hole becomes the "swineherd."

Quail Without a Tail

This game involves a chant that in Polish refers to the crow, because that word in Polish rhymes with the word for tail. We have changed it here to "quail" because it is necessary to have the rhyme, and to make it more of a tongue twister in English.

Directions:

Two children sit opposite each other with their arms crossed. They alternate in saying the following chant as fast as they can, until one stumbles and the game is finished, or they start over again until they are tired of the game.

> *First quail without a tail,*
> *Second quail without a tail,*
> *Third quail without a tail,*
> *Fourth quail without a tail,*
> *Fifth quail without a tail,*

[continue on with successive numbers]

Dyngus or Dingus

This is a very old custom, dating to the Middle Ages. Nowadays it is treated more as a game, and it sometimes gets out of hand. Traditionally, in some areas of Poland the boys and young men tried to softly whip the girls using a branch of pussy willows instead of splashing them with water. However, today water is used in most parts of Poland.

Directions:

1. Early on the morning of Easter Monday, boys and young men prepare bottles of water or squirt guns, or any container from which they can easily splash water.

2. They search out the girls in their family or among their friends and sprinkle or spray them with water, often chanting a rhyme. (In the Polish American community of Pine Creek, Wisconsin, where Anne Pellowski grew up, the chant was *Dyngus, dyngus, po dwa jaja; nie chce chleba tylko jaja.* ["Dyngus, dyngus, for two eggs; I don't want bread but eggs."] A further description can be found in the chapter "Dyngus" in *Stairstep Farm.*)

3. If the boy or young man succeeds in getting a girl wet, he can ask a forfeit, in many cases a decorated real egg or a chocolate one—or perhaps even a kiss!

4. On Easter Tuesday, the roles are reversed, with the girls trying to splash or squirt water on the boys.

Seasonal Activities

The Green Leaf

This game is very old. It is played primarily with friends, not strangers. The trick is to catch people at moments when they are less likely to have a green leaf, such as when coming out of the bathroom, during a church service, or while attending a formal function of some sort.

In spring, after the first leaves have appeared on trees, one must carry a green leaf somewhere on one's person. Any friend one chances to meet may ask: "Where is your green leaf?" If the first person does not have such a leaf, he or she is forced to pay a small forfeit or offer to do a favor.

Lanie Wosku (Pouring Wax)

This activity always takes place on Saint Andrew's Day, November 30. The participants form a circle. A large washbowl of cool water is placed in the center of the circle. Each person gets a small lighted candle (or one candle is passed from person to person).

One by one, each person in the circle drips a small amount of wax into the water. The rest of the group "interprets" the shapes and pretends to predict what the shape means for the future of the person who poured the wax. The fun is in seeing unusual shapes in the wax and inventing wild predictions, the more exaggerated the better.

Marzanna

This activity dates to pagan times and is a relic of the idea of "getting rid of winter," which is also a symbol of getting rid of death. Marzanna takes place on March 21, or on the fourth Sunday of Lent, called Laetare Sunday, depending on the local custom.

Young girls, and in some areas adult women as well, make life-sized dolls of straw. They are usually dressed in old clothes representing the dress of that area. The girls and women march in procession to a nearby river, singing special songs. Upon reaching the river, the doll is thrown into the water, and a typical verse is recited. The group then pick a small branch with green leaves, decorate it with ribbons, and come back to the starting point (home or school). Singing songs that indicate they have gotten rid of death, they sometimes pass from house to house and are given treats.

Wianki (Wreaths)

Wreaths are made for many occasions, but two have special meaning: on June 21, known as Saint John's Eve, and during the harvest festival known as *dozynki*, usually in late August.

For Saint John's Eve celebrations, girls make wreaths of common flowers such as daisies, dahlias, and zinnias. These wreaths are thrown into the water in the direction the current is flowing. In some places, young men wait in groups at the edge of the river, each hoping to catch the wreath made by the girl he wishes to get to know better. It is not uncommon to have a young man propose marriage after plucking a girl's wreath out of the water—so he had better have the right one!

During *dozynki*, the wreaths were usually made of stalks of the grains harvested, rather than flowers. This festival was of great importance to the Kaszubians and survived in such areas as Pine Creek and Stevens Point, both in Wisconsin, and in Winona, Minnesota, where large groups of Kaszubians settled. The wreath was made in a crown shape and decorated with ribbons. It was worn by a young girl who had taken part in the harvest, or was given by a husband to his wife, to wear while eating the feast of special foods celebrating the end of harvesting.

Other occasions for wreath making include name days and for a bride to be, before or during the wedding.

RIDDLES

These are only a few of the hundreds of traditional riddles extant in Poland. Of course, Polish children today have modern invented riddles similar to North American children's riddles, based on silly puns or on conventions such as "Knock, knock. Who's there?"

There is a forest; below the forest, some lookers; below the lookers, some breathers; below the breathers, some snappers; below the snappers, some grabbers; below the grabbers, some ballooners; below the ballooners, some kneelers; below the kneelers, some stampers.

Answer: Hair, eyes, nose, mouth and teeth, belly and guts, knees, feet

Black blinks; white bites.

Answer: Eyes and teeth

It is nothing, and yet we can see it.

Answer: A shadow

The First, I don't remember; the Second, I did not feel; the Third, I do not know.

Answer: My birth, my growing up, my hour of death.

He walks through the field searching for something he did not lose.

Answer: A hunter

Two sons and two fathers went hunting. They caught only three rabbits, and yet each went home with one. How can this be?

Answer: Grandfather, father, and son went hunting

Four standers, two sticks, and a rope. What is it?

Answer: An ox

It was born in a tiny hole but can walk up mountains. What is it?

Answer: A mouse

I was born red; I came up green; I was cut white and taken to the grave. What am I?

Answer: A grain of rye

There is a wee pen made of three brown boards, and inside the pen is a tiny white ox ready to burst out. What is it?

Answer: A grain of buckwheat

Here comes a little fellow with a hundred coats. You help him take them off, and he makes you cry.

Answer: An onion

A white pillowcase with no seams. What is it?

Answer: An egg

A red bead with the flavor of wine but a heart of stone. What is it?

Answer: A cherry

A round loaf of golden bread sits among millions of silver peas. What are they?

Answer: The moon and stars

An ox bellows far away beyond a hundred hills, and yet we hear him plainly. What is it?

Answer: Thunder

You take more and more out, but you don't have more, you have less. What is it?

Answer: A hole

Red splashes on top, black on the bottom. What is it?

Answer: Fire

A gray horse runs up to the heavens. What is it?

Answer: Smoke

Black grains on a white field. What is it?

Answer: Writing

It does not eat, it does not drink, but it can go along and give a loud bang so that it can scare you. What is it?

Answer: A grandfather clock

What runs away and never comes back?

Answer: Time

Three horses have one tail. What is it?

Answer: A fork

In summer, a stranger; in winter, our darling friend. What is it?

Answer: A stove

Four brothers are they, all looking alike; they lead each other a merry chase. Yet never does one catch up to the next, and never does one see the other's face. What is it?

Answer: A traditional windmill with four arms

He goes to the field and knocks down everything, but doesn't pick it up. What is it?

Answer: A scythe

It isn't greased, but it goes. What is it?

Answer: A sleigh (This riddle is actually a kind of pun on a famous saying in Poland, "Who greases, goes.")

NURSERY RHYMES

All of the nursery rhymes here have been translated with great liberty. The aim was to give the same sense of rhythm and rhyme, rather than a literal translation of the words. We have included the original Polish words for some of them in the "Sources," for those who wish to use them with Polish American children.

Magpie Cooked a Pot of Porridge

This is a finger rhyme. The directions for the appropriate actions are given after each line in the rhyme. Because the word "magpie" is not as well known to young children in the United States, it is acceptable to substitute the word "blackbird."

Magpie cooked a pot of porridge.
[Make a stirring motion in one palm of child's hand.]

Gave it to the girls (boys) to eat.
[Use whichever there are most of in the family.]

The first he fed from a cup.
[Gently wiggle little finger of child's hand.]

The second with a teaspoon he gave to sup.
[Wiggle ring finger.]

To the third he passed a mug.
[Wiggle middle finger.]

The fourth got all the rest in a jug.
[Wiggle index finger.]

The fifth little one he tapped on the head.
[Tap thumb on top of head.]

And then—frrrrr—
Into the woods the magpie fled.
[Adult puts hand into baby's hair or mother's hair. Some put hand into armpit of baby.]

Little Kittens

This rhyme has many, many variants. Sometimes it is accompanied by the movements of the adult hands, guiding the child's two hands, pretending to be the kittens, or clapping gently. It is one of the first rhymes little Polish children learn by heart.

Shoo! Shoo! Shoo!
Little kittens two.
Both are brown and gray.
They're not doing anything;
Just wishing _____ would play.
[Fill in name of child.]

Off to Grandma and Grandpa

Another rhyme learned by almost every little child. Sometimes it is done simply as a clapping rhyme; in other cases it is accompanied by rocking or by lifting the child rhythmically up and down on the knees. The rhyme can go on and on, with each verse having different things in the last two lines, provided they give a semblance of rhyming.

Clap, clap your little paws;
We are off to Grandma's house.
Gran gives milk when we awake;
Grandpa gives us honey cake.
Clap, clap your little hands;
We are off to Grandpa's lands.
Grandma gives us porridge, hot.
Grandpa gives us sugar, a lot.

The Crab

This rhyme is concerned with the different parts of the body. It is a means of introducing the very young child to the names for the hands, legs, nose, mouth, ears, and other parts of the body. Such rhymes are common in many cultures. Make sure the pinching is more like a gentle tweaking than a true pinch.

Here comes a little pinching crab.
[Adult moves thumb and index finger in a gentle pinch.]
Wherever he goes, he makes a grab!
[Pinch hair on baby's head.]

He goes far.
[Pinch fingers on one hand.]
Then he goes near.
[Pinch fingers on other hand.]
He goes there to an ear.
[Pinch one ear.]
Then he moves over here.
[Pinch other ear.]
To the mouth like a rose.
[Pinch mouth.]
To the pink bellybutton.
[Pinch bellybutton.]
Then down to the toes.
[Pinch toes.]
And then up that crab goes.
[Move hand up to face of child.]
To pinch little _____ 's nose.
[Insert name of child and pinch nose.]

The Ladybug

This is another finger rhyme.

A ladybug so bright and red,
Met some worms on the bed.
She said "Hi" to the one that was fat.
[Touch thumb of child.]
To the second she gave a pat.
[Touch index finger.]
To the third she gave a shake.
[Shake middle finger.]
This one she pulled and tried to take.
[Gently pull on ring finger.]
To this little one she said "Good-bye."
[Wave little finger back and forth.]
And then flew off, up into the sky.
[Adult hand moves up and away.]

Old Man Tease

In the original the man is named Roch, to rhyme with the Polish word for peas, which is *groch*. The rest of the rhyme pretty much follows the sense of the Polish original. Peas, especially hard yellow dried peas, are a staple of Polish cooking.

Old man Tease, sowed some peas.
As he sowed, how he glowed.
As he reaped, how he leaped.
As he threshed, he felt refreshed.
As he cooked them in a pot, his hands and fingers got so hot.
As he ate, not one did he miss, and his heart was full of bliss.

Off to Market

This is an endless rhyme, similar to the idea of "Ninety-nine Bottles of Beer" in English. One keeps going for as long as the audience will listen. In the original, the man is named Marek to rhyme with the word for town market or fair.

Off to market on his feet, without his cart went farmer Pete.
Bought an axle, size just right; put it in his barn, upright.
Someone stole it in the night.
Said his neighbor, one of the men: "Go to market once again.
Buy another axle and then . . ."
Off to market on his feet, without his cart went farmer Pete.
Bought another, size just right; put it in his barn, upright.
Someone stole it in the night.
Said his neighbor, one of the men: "Go to market once again.
Buy another axle, and then . . ."
Off to market on his feet, without his cart went farmer Pete.
Bought a third, size just right, put it in his barn, upright.
Someone stole it in the night.

[Continue until begged to stop.]

Where Is the Wolf?

This rhyme is either simply recited, with the adult pretending to "eat" the child's body by kissing it in many places, or someone performs the actions stated here. This rhyme is also used by older children when playing a circle game.

Where is the wolf? Running in the hills.
What is he doing? Chasing the geese.
Has he found many? More than twenty.
How are his eyes?
Like coals in the night skies. [Form circles around eyes.]
How are his ears?
Like spears that one fears. [Point a finger above each ear.]
How is his nose?
Like the end of a hose. [Make circle around nose.]
How are his front paws?
Like wood-cutting saws. [Move arms in saw-cutting motion.]
How are his hind legs?
Like two huge wooden pegs. [Move legs stiffly.]
How is his snout?
Big! The better to eat you, no doubt! [Make smacking noises all over child's body.]

PART 3

Local Legends

LECH, CECH, AND RUS

This is a short version of a very old legend. It is known throughout Poland. Cech is an early spelling of Czech and is pronounced the same. Rus is pronounced "Roose" to rhyme with moose. In some versions, the three are not brothers, but rather cousins or simply knights.

*M*ore than a thousand years ago, there lived three brothers. Their names were Lech, Cech, and Rus. After their father died, they wandered off for several years. When they got homesick, they all set off for home. They all met on the same day and in the same place. Each shouted at the same time: "Poznaje!" which means "I know you!" And afterward, that place was called Poznan.

But the brothers did not always get along. They went to live in different areas. Lech's territory was to the west of Rus's. Cech's territory was to the south of Lech's and Rus's. They started fighting each other and invading each other's lands.

One day Lech was out riding on his horse when, in the distance, he saw a mother eagle, circling over her nest. He knew that if he could get near the nest and capture one of those young eagles, he would be able to train it to hunt for him.

Lech approached the nest cautiously, but the mother eagle saw him and attacked him with her beak and wings and claws. No matter from which side he approached, the mother eagle spied him and attacked him if he got too near the nest. She defended it with all the power she had. But if Lech did not approach too closely, she did not attack him or even come near him. She allowed him to ride in peace all around it.

The longer Lech tried to approach the nest, the more it made him think of the land he was always trying to protect. And Cech and Rus, also, wanted mostly to protect their lands. Lech called a truce and invited Cech and Rus to his domain. He told them of his experience with the mother eagle.

"We must each act like that mother eagle," said Lech. "If we agree on which territory is out nest territory and respect each other's "nests," we will be able to spend time building our homes instead of destroying them."

All three made a pact, and each went back to his "nest" territory. For a long time there was peace in those lands. Lech became the ruler of Lechia, which is now called Poland.

Cech became the ruler of the territory that is now part of the Czech Republic, and Rus became the ruler of the land we now call Russia.

And ever since that time, the eagle has been the symbol of Poland, the desire it expressed to protect its nest territory, and the promise not to fight for more. In honor of that mother eagle, the first capital of Lechia was called Gniezno, which means "nest." It is one of the oldest cities in Poland. And Lech remains one of the most beloved names in Poland.

KING POPIEL

This legend follows directly after the one above, after the time of Lech, approximately 850 C.E. There is some historical evidence for the existence of this king. The Mouse Tower in the town of Kruszwica, which is very close to the first capital, Gniezno, is all that is left of the castle where King Popiel reigned. However, that tower is known to have been built long after the supposed reign of King Popiel. This legend has been the source of a number of po-ems by well-known poets, among them Julius Slowacki and Czeslaw Milosz. Milosz pub-lished a rather ironic poem called "King Popiel" as the lead selection in his poetry collection, d Krol Popiel I Inne Wiersze (1962).

A few hundred years after Lech, King Popiel I had a son. In time he became King Popiel II and ruled in Poland. He did not wish to be identified with Lech, so he moved the capital to Kruszwica, a nearby town, and there he built a castle of bricks and stone, with a round tower at the side. It stood at the edge of Lake Goplo.

King Popiel II was not a wise ruler, and the people did not like him. He was cruel and lived a life of extravagant feasting and drinking. He had a large number of uncles, and he was always fearful that they would attempt to overthrow him. King Popiel and his wife decided to get rid of the uncles for good.

They arranged for a huge feast and invited all the uncles and their courtiers. During the feast, the uncles began to fall over, one by one. They could not believe what was happening to them. They had all been poisoned by Popiel and his wife. Before they died, some of the uncles cursed Popiel and said he would not reign much longer. But Popiel and his wife paid no attention and just enjoyed their success in getting rid of all those who wanted to take away his kingship.

Suddenly they heard a squeaking and pattering of feet from Lake Goplo. When they looked out, they saw thousands of mice crawling up the castle walls. They smelled of death, and their whiskers stood straight out as they showed their sharp teeth. They advanced on Popiel and his wife, who tried to stomp on them and kill them, but there were just too many. King Popiel and the queen escaped to the tower and climbed to the very top, shutting and locking the great door. They thought they were safe. But the mice advanced relentlessly, gnawing their way through the wood. Soon they had worked their way into the tower room. There were sounds of a fearful struggle.

After a short while the mice departed from the castle, returning to Lake Goplo. When the frightened people of Kruszwica dared to enter the castle, they found the bodies of Popiel's uncles lying dead in the great hall. When they went up to the tower room, there was nothing there but a few pieces of royal cloth and a few jewels that the queen had been wearing. Not a trace of King Popiel and his wife remained.

THE FOUNDING OF THE PIAST DYNASTY

There is some historical evidence for the life of Ziemowit Piast, but the legends that grew up around him are far more numerous than the actual historical references. He is believed to have restored the capital to Gniezno.

*I*n the town of Gniezno, while Popiel was still king, there was a prince who was about to have the coming-of-age ceremony for his two sons. During that ceremony, the sons would have their hair cut off for the first time to signify that they were young men, not boys. The whole town seemed to be celebrating this happy event.

Two travelers arrived at the palace gates. They wore old clothes that were dirty from their long travels, and they were very hungry. They asked to come in and share the food and drink, but the guards refused to let them in. The travelers begged to be allowed to rest for a while, but the guards and family of the prince, fearful they were there to harm the young princes, turned them away with nothing, and even called them thieves. The two wandered on to the edge of the town, and there they came upon the home of Piast, a ploughman working the lands of the prince. Piast stood in front of his humble cottage, and next to him stood his son. As soon as Piast saw the two travelers, he realized they were tired and hungry. He invited them in and asked them to rest while his wife prepared some food. As soon as it was ready, they sat down to eat. But the amazing thing was, as soon as the food had been cleared from the serving platter, more of the same appeared.

"Do you have something for us to drink?" asked the travelers.

"Yes," answered Piast. "I have saved up to buy a keg of beer, for soon my son will have his coming-of-age ceremony, just like the princes, and I wished to have some to offer to my guests. But you are welcome to share it with us now." He served each of the travelers a mug of beer. The same thing happened to the keg of beer that had happened to the food. As soon as some of the beer was served, the keg filled up again.

When Piast and his wife saw this miracle, they asked the travelers if they should invite the prince and his family to share in the ceremony at their home. The travelers agreed it would be a fine idea, and then they went on their way.

Piast invited the prince, his family, and all the noble families to join them in their celebration as well. He assured them he would have enough to eat and drink. Which, indeed, they did have, for whatever they had prepared to eat was soon replenished, as though no one had taken a bite. And the keg of beer never grew empty. The prince himself cut the hair of Piast's son, and he was given the name Ziemowit, which some say means "welcomed throughout the land." Ziemowit grew up to be a knight, and when Popiel was no longer king, he helped to save Poland from an invasion and was named king. And thus began the Piast dynasty.

THE DRAGON OF WAWEL

Krakow is first mentioned in written history in about 965 C.E. It was already a major trading city. Even though it was the capital only through the sixteenth century, all Polish kings were crowned there until the eighteenth century.

*L*ong ago there was a high hill along the Vistula River in southern Poland that was filled with caves. In one of the caves lived a dragon. It lay sleeping there for many years. The people of the town surrounding the hill knew that the dragon was there, for it had attacked in the past; they feared the day it would awaken again.

One day, some young people from the town decided to go exploring the caves, against their parents' wishes. They came upon the dragon, and with their frightened screams, woke it up. It roared, and out of its mouth came blistering flames. Through the flames, they could see its red eyes and sharp white teeth. They ran as fast as they could, back down to their homes. But now the dragon was awake and very hungry. It snatched up a cow from a field and swallowed it whole.

Every day after that, the dragon came out, searching for animals to eat. If there were none in the foothills, it would approach the town. The townspeople got tired of sending their cows, sheep, and goats to the fields to graze, only to have them disappear into the mouth of the dragon. They tried different ways to kill the dragon or put it to sleep again, but none of them succeeded.

At last a young man named Krakus decided to try. He had learned how to use minerals and plants to create different potions and medicines. He stirred up a vat full of sulfur, tar, and poisonous liquids. This he smeared on the carcasses of several dead sheep. He left them near the entrance to the dragon's cave.

When the dragon came out, it devoured the sheep quickly and looked around for more to eat. Soon the minerals and poisons began to react inside the dragon's belly. They burned and bubbled and itched. The dragon felt as though it was on fire inside. It crawled to the Vistula River and began to drink. The water inside the dragon began to boil and bubble and burn all the more. The dragon drank and drank and drank until it could drink no more, and then it burst into a thousand pieces.

The people were so happy to get rid of the dragon, they asked Krakus to be their ruler. In his honor, they changed the name of their town to Krakow. They built him a castle on top of the hill that they called Wawel. It is still there today.

QUEEN WANDA

This is certainly one of the best-known legends in Poland, and its popularity reached beyond Poland's borders. The Czech composer Antonin Dvorak used it as the basis for his opera, Wanda. In one variant or other, it can be found in most language textbooks in present-day Poland.

King Krakus reigned happily for many years. He married and had three children, two sons and a daughter. When Krakus grew old and then died, the oldest son, Krak, was ready to be crowned the next king. But his youngest brother was jealous, and one day, in a fit of anger, he killed his brother Krak.

For a short time no one suspected what he had done, and he ruled on the throne as king. But then his evil deed was discovered, and he fled to the deepest forest in Poland, hoping to escape justice.

Now only the daughter of Krakus remained. Her name was Wanda, and she had grown up to be wise and kind and brave. At first she did not wish to be queen, but finally she was persuaded it was the only way to bring peace to her country. She ruled with wisdom and understanding for a few years.

Then came alarming news. A Germanic ruler from lands to the west was threatening to attack. His name was Prince Rytygier, and he had been assembling a large army for some time. Queen Wanda called her knights together and, leaving only a few behind to defend Krakow, she led them in a surprise attack on Prince Rytygier's army. They succeeded in pushing back his forces so they were not so near.

Prince Rytygier did not regard this as a defeat, but as a challenge. He still wanted the rich lands and the wealth of the Polish crown. Furthermore, he had seen that Queen Wanda was as beautiful as she was fearless. He assembled an army greater than any that had ever been seen in that part of the world. He positioned his troops all around Queen Wanda's territory and then sent a messenger with his ultimatum: She must marry him and join their kingdoms together, or he would attack and destroy her land and all the people in it.

The courtiers in Wawel waited anxiously to hear what Queen Wanda's reply would be. Many of her counselors advised her to accept.

At last Queen Wanda had her answer ready and she sent it to Prince Rytygier: "I could never marry a ruler such as you. You want to live by ruthless force. I wish to live in peace. I am ready to give up my life rather than be forced to marry against my will, to one who can only bring sorrow to our land."

Prince Rytygier was astounded. The earliest written histories say that he was so overcome with shame and sorrow, he took his own life. Later historians wrote that Wanda did indeed sacrifice herself for her people, by leaping into the Vistula River. No matter which story is believed, Polish people honor Queen Wanda as a symbol of right standing up to might.

THE TRUMPETER OF KRAKOW

The date of the Tartar invasion mentioned in this tale is probably 1241. There is no written historical record that verifies the account of the trumpeter, but it has been passed down orally for centuries. The legend was made known to a worldwide audience after the publication of The Trumpeter of Krakow, by Eric Kelly, in 1928. The book won the Newbery award and was translated into many languages. It is still the best version of the story, for it gives much more of the historical context than can be included here.

*F*or a number of years, Poland was threatened by invasions from the Tartars from the east. The Tartars came in large troops, carrying the bows and arrows for which they were famous. They had already conquered much of the lands now known as Russia, Bulgaria, Romania, and Hungary. Poland would surely be next. Watchmen were sent to watch from the highest points in the city of Krakow, the most likely place for the invaders to attack Poland.

One day a watchman saw in the distance a huge cloud of dust. It was moving in the direction of Krakow. The watchman could think of only one thing to do. Raising his trumpet to his mouth, he played a short fanfare, sending it in all directions over the city. He played it over and over. At first the people were puzzled, but then they realized they would soon be attacked. Their best archers took up positions on the battlements that protected the city.

When the Tartars drew near, they were met with a hail of arrows from the Polish defenders. Wave after wave, the horde of Tartars came storming up to the city wall, and flying to meet them were the arrows from the Polish archers. Through it all, the trumpeter kept playing, calling everyone to arms.

But the Tartars had very skillful archers. One of them saw the trumpeter and took aim. The arrow flew right at the watchman, and the music stopped in the middle of a note. But the Polish defenders continued to fight. One of their arrows killed the Tartar leader, and they were all forced to retreat. When the people went up to the watchtower, they found the watchman lying there dead. An arrow had pierced his throat.

Poland was saved, and the people wanted to remember that brave watchman. In his honor, they played the same fanfare, the *hejnal*, from the tower of St. Mary's church in the central square of Krakow. Since that time it is played four times each hour, in the four directions, twenty-four hours each day. And the men of the Krakow fire brigade who have the responsibility for playing the trumpet always break off in the middle of a note, just as that watchman did so many years ago.

THE WARSAW MERMAID

Warsaw, the present capital of Poland, is nowhere near the sea. Why, then, does it have a mermaid as its symbol, set in its coat of arms, a fact well documented from about 1600 onward? There are basically two legends answering this question, each with many variants. The lack of historical evidence for either does not trouble the citizens of Warsaw, who love their mermaid and have used it as a symbol of resistance to oppression. Pictures of the mermaid can be seen everywhere in Warsaw. She is shown with a raised sword in her right hand and a round shield in her left. There are two statues of the mermaid in the city, one of them recently moved to the center square of the Old Town. The pronunciation of the two parts of the name are "Var" and "Shava."

First Version

A very long time ago a nobleman from the region of Mazovia went out hunting on his extensive property. He saw a strange beast and was about to shoot it with his bow and arrow, but it disappeared. He tried to find it again, walking here and there. His walking made him very thirsty so he went to the edge of the Vistula River and began to drink. To his amazement, there in the water appeared a mermaid.

"You must follow the path the arrow has taken, along the river," she said.

The prince walked in the direction in which the arrow had flown, and suddenly he came upon a small village. He entered the first cottage he came to, because he was hungry and wanted to ask for food. There by the fire sat a young woman with twin babies, a boy and a girl. The woman shared her food with the nobleman and then they went into the front garden to talk. When the nobleman asked the woman what her babies were called, she said they had not yet been named.

"You must call the boy War and the girl Sawa," said the nobleman. "And because you have been so generous with your food, I grant you this land all along the river. From now on, it is yours."

At that moment, the mermaid raised her head from the waters of the Vistula and chanted: "Your village will grow and grow, never fear; in the future a beautiful city will be here."

And so it was, for that site became the city of Warsaw. And the nobleman insisted that the symbol for the city be the mermaid who had predicted it.

Second Version

There was a nobleman who went on a visit to the Baltic Sea. While swimming in the sea, he met a mermaid and fell in love with her. He took her back to live with him in Warsaw, where he kept her in a secret pool in his palace.

When the Swedes attacked in the middle of the sixteenth century, the nobleman fought with his countrymen. The mermaid came out of hiding and took up one of her husband's swords and shields. Then she joined him in the fight. The Swedish warriors were so astounded, they fell back in defeat. Shortly after that, the mermaid became the symbol of resistance for all of Warsaw.

BAZYLISZEK

This legend certainly was derived from the Greek legend of the basilisk. In its Polish version, the legend is always set in Warsaw, and the figure has a distinct look. In most European versions, the green and yellow lizardlike figure is said to have been hatched from a giant egg, laid by a rooster!

A long, long time ago, huge dungeons were dug out under Warsaw, to help in defending the city. Soon one of them was taken over by Bazyliszek, a giant lizard who had a huge red crest, like a rooster's, on the top of its head. People lived in fear of the Bazyliszek because if you accidentally looked at it, you dropped down dead at the first glance.

One day a young sister and brother went to the annual fair in Warsaw. They saw jugglers and dancers. They saw a man eat fire! The little sister saw the many beautiful and shiny things for sale, and begged her brother, Anthony, to buy something for her. He had very little money, but at last he agreed to buy her a small mirror.

They kept walking along, and soon Anthony realized they were in a part of the city he had never seen before. They were standing next to a strange looking house, with a red door and an iron knocker that looked as though it were a large dragon ready to pounce on someone. The door was slightly open, and Anthony decided to take a look inside. It was so dark that he could see nothing. Rather than open the door wider, he decided to take the mirror he had bought for his little sister and hold it in such a way that it would reflect sunlight into the dark beyond the doorway.

He held the mirror just so, and there, in the mirror, he saw the horrible Bazyliszek, with its green and yellow scales, its glowing red eyes, and its rooster comb sticking straight up. He had heard of that terrible monster. He was so frightened, he took his sister by the hand, and they ran home as fast as they could.

Their family was very poor, and even worse times came. They had nothing to eat. Anthony thought and thought about the Bazyliszek. He knew it was a horrible monster, but he had heard that it guarded an enormous treasure in its dungeon under Warsaw. He determined to go to that strange house once again, to see if he could get some of the gold.

Taking his little sister's mirror, he set off. He soon found the strange house with the red door. Again, the door was slightly open. Holding the mirror in front of him, and looking only at it, he entered the dungeon. There in the mirror he saw Bazyliszek, sound asleep. At its feet were heaped gold coins and jewels. Anthony took some of the gold coins , but in trying to put them into his pocket, they made a clinking sound. Bazyliszek awoke!

Quickly Anthony held out the mirror, right in front of Bazyliszek's eyes. The monster took one look at itself in the mirror, gave a piercing scream, and fell over dead. Anthony gathered as many coins as he could carry and then went out into the streets of Warsaw to tell everyone the good news. Bazyliszek was dead.

THE SLEEPING KNIGHTS

This motif is common in other parts of Europe as well. In Poland it is usually tied to the knights of King Boleslaw, crowned in 1025 as the first king of greater Poland. The legend has numerous versions. In many of them, the point of view is that of a blacksmith who is called to shoe the horses every now and then. When the tale was written down in the late 1890s as told by the famous storyteller Sabala (see Stopka in the bibliography), he narrated it as though it had happened to one of his blacksmith friends.

*I*n the valley of Koscielisko, in the Tatra mountains, there is a high peak that resembles the head of a sleeping warrior. Inside that peak is a hidden cavern, a huge one, with a spring that flows out into the Dunajec River.

One day a shepherd following his sheep saw in the distance an opening in the mountainside from which water flowed. He tried to get to the opening, but the water was icy cold. Nevertheless, he decided to enter at any cost and cut across the stream. Cold and shivering, he entered the mountain and saw a deep valley spread before him. As is common among the shepherds of the Tatras, he yodeled into the valley. The echo came back to him. He yodeled a second time, and back came the echo again. He yodeled a third time and then stood frozen on the spot. Instead of an echo, he heard the sound of organ music. There was no church nearby. From where did the music come?

Suddenly there appeared before him a figure covered in armor, with a helmet on his head and wings on his shoulders. He carried a broad sword in his right hand. The knight stood there, looking as golden as the sun, and spoke to the shepherd.

"Who goes by here, so bold as to wake us up from our sleep? Is it time to get up and march?"

The shepherd, dumbfounded and frightened, replied that he was not there to make trouble. He did not understand the knight's questions. The knight, noticing the shepherd's fear, said, "Don't be afraid. No harm will come to you. I am not a robber, but a soldier. My blood was shed for my country, and after that my fellow soldiers and I have been put to sleep here in this rocky mountain. The time will come for us to fight for faith and country once again. When that time comes, a young man such as you will find a way to wake thousands, perhaps even a million of us. He will arrive at the entryway and call out in his loudest voice: 'Awake, knights, awake from your long-lasting sleep. Awake and go down among the people. Go to their aid, just like angels from heaven'."

The shepherd listened to the knight as if in a trance. He fell down on his knees in front of the knight and said, "I will help you, even though I might have to go to the ends of the earth."

The knight lifted the shepherd from the ground and told him that he would know his duty. He would show him what he must do, and with the evidence of his own eyes, the shepherd would believe in his task. The knight took him deeper into the cave, until they came to a cavern that shone with a bright light. It was so vast it took them several hours to pass through and see it all. It was a hundred times bigger than any other cave in Poland. The walls seemed to have strange shapes. There were no plants of any kind.

When the shepherd accidentally touched the knight, the sound of a tremendous organ filled the cavern. The shepherd then saw a chapel off to one side. It had a glittering stone altar. Beside it was a fountain that looked as though it had been turned to stone. Finally, the shepherd perceived before him something he had never before imagined in his life. There in the chapel and beyond were row after row of knights/soldiers in helmets, outfitted differently, and each one having wings on his shoulders. Some wore costumes of leopard, lion, or tiger skins. Others had shining armor. Their horses were decorated with clusters of white feathers, and they all had golden horseshoes.

The shepherd gave a small cry of surprise, and the knights began to shake themselves awake. When the knight accompanying the shepherd saw the soldiers moving, he called out sharply, "Not yet!" The soldiers settled once again into their positions, like stone statues. The knight took his place beside them, but before he turned back to stone, he commanded the shepherd to return to his home by the same route.

"Never return here," he ordered. "Never search for this place again, for you will not find it, unless you are called upon to wake us in time of need."

After a loud crashing noise, the shepherd found himself at a golden gate. He fell to the ground, and the rocks and everything around him seemed to be spinning. He picked himself up and started walking toward his home. He wondered if all he had seen had been a dream.

The shepherd grew up to be a wise old man. He thought many times of the things he might have seen as a young man, but he never longed to go back up to the spot on the mountain where he had entered the cave. And he never heard, during his lifetime, the call that would have told him he must go and wake the sleeping knights: "Now is the time!"

PAN TWARDOWSKI

This tale is known in all areas of Poland. The place-names are all real and usually do not change even though other parts of the tale might be different in other versions. The first full written version seems to date to the early nineteenth century, but there are many references to it before that. It has been illustrated countless times. There is a mirror housed in a church in Wegrow, dating to approximately 1706, with a legend attached that states it was the mirror used by Pan Twardowski while accomplishing some of his evil deeds. Be sure to re-read the note about Pan, Pani, and Panna in part 1.

*P*an Twardowski was a fine young man, of noble birth on both his mother's and father's side. He wanted to have more wisdom, more than other people seemed to desire. He decided to find out if there was a medicine that would prevent death from coming. He really did not want to die.

In an old book, he read how one could summon up the devil and make a contract. He decided to try it. One midnight, he slipped out of Krakow where he was living and searching for the cure for death. He went to the foot of a mountain, near the town of Podgorze. He called out to the devil in a loud voice.

The devil came at once, as though he were accustomed to being there, and he carried a contract. After discussing the terms, the devil used his knee as a desk and wrote them out. Pan Twardowski had to sign the contract with his own blood, which he got by pricking his ring finger. The principal clause of the contract was this: The devil would be Twardowski's servant all his life, but when he died, he would belong to the devil. However, the devil would have no claim on Twardowski's body or soul unless he caught him in Rome.

Now, Pan Twardowski commanded, "Collect all the silver to be found in Poland and find a spot there to bury it safely under a thin layer of earth." As Twardowski said this, he pointed in the direction of Olkusz. The devil obeyed, and that is why there have been rich veins of silver ore in and around Olkusz since that time.

Pan Twardowski made his second request: "Bring a huge rock to this cliff and show me you can balance it on its tip in such a way that it will never fall down." The devil obeyed, and to this very day the rock stands at a place called Pieskowa Skala, which means "rock." But the rock itself is called "Falcon's Rock."

Everything that Pan Twardowski wanted, at any time, the devil had to grant. Twardowski became famous as a magician. If he saw a canvas of painted horses and wanted to ride them, all he had to do was wish for it, and the horses came running out of the picture, ready for him to ride. To go faster, he would climb on the back of a giant rooster and it would take him far away, faster than any horse. He went out on the Vistula River with young women he fancied, and the boat glided swiftly along, without sails or oars. He could take a piece of glass in his hand and start a fire in a village a hundred miles away.

One day he took such a fancy to a young girl that he decided to marry her. But the girl was very particular. She came from a well-off family and was not going to marry just anyone. She let it be known that in a stone jar she had put a living thing, and only the person who could guess what it was would have her hand in marriage.

Pan Twardowski came to call on her, dressed as a beggar. He asked to see the stone jar.

The girl stepped forward and said:

"What is this creature, tiny or long?

You'll be my husband if you don't guess wrong."

Pan Twardowski, with the help of the power the devil had given him, saw right through the stone of the jar. He answered her:

"It is a bee, dear little lady.

Upon my life, you must now be my wife."

Pan Twardowski hid his wealth from his wife. He had many manor houses, but he forced her to live in a hut in a corner of Krakow. He did not want her to gain power over him in some way. She became a potter and lived by selling her pots in the central market. But often Twardowski's servants would pass by and stomp on the pots, shattering them into small pieces.

Gold passed through Pan Twardowski's hands as though it were sand, because any time he wanted more, the devil brought it. But the devil was getting anxious. One day, as Twardowski was walking in a forest near Krakow, the devil jumped out at him and yelled, "It's time you went to Rome!" The devil was so angry, he uprooted a tree and gave a whack at one of Twardowski's legs. After that, Pan Twardowski always walked with a limp.

Many more years passed, and the devil simply got tired of waiting for Twardowski to go to Rome. He disguised himself as a courtier attached to the court of a foreign nobleman, being careful to wear a large hat that covered his horns. He went to Twardowski and said, in the saddest voice he could muster, "My master is dying in an inn nearby. He needs a healer and asks that you come. He has heard of your magical powers and will reward you handsomely if you help him."

Pan Twardowski went, not realizing that the inn was called the "Rome Inn." The moment he stepped inside, a swarm of crows, ravens, and owls swooped down and sat on the roof. They began squawking and screeching so loudly that the sounds filled the inn. Twardowski recognized the signs that the devil was near and guessed what might happen. In a corner of the room he spied a baby in a cradle, being guarded by a nursemaid. The baby was wearing a lovely white gown as though it had just been baptized. Twardowski snatched up the infant and held on to it tightly. He began shaking like an aspen leaf.

At that moment the devil stepped into the inn, dressed in the finest of clothes: a three-cornered hat, a frock coat, a long vest to cover his belly, tight trousers, silk stockings, and shoes with silver buckles. But everyone knew it was the devil because the three-cornered hat did not hide his horns. The devil approached Twardowski, ready to take him away. But then he noticed the newborn baby, dressed in the christening outfit. He ordered Twardowski to put it back into the cradle, but he would not do so.

"Are you not a true nobleman?" asked the devil. "A nobleman's word must always be kept." The devil even quoted the saying in Latin. Then he continued, "You signed a contract, swearing by your blood that you would come with me if you ever went to Rome. This inn is called Rome. So you must come with me."

Twardowski knew that as a nobleman he could not break his word. He put the baby back in its cradle. No sooner had he done that than the devil grabbed him and they flew up the chimney. The owls, ravens, and crows screamed and squawked and swarmed around them. Higher and higher they flew. Twardowski looked down and saw the earth below. Villages looked like tiny gnats. Krakow looked no bigger than two spiders sitting next to each other. They flew high above the Carpathian Mountains, where no vultures or eagles could reach them.

Suddenly Pan Twardowski began to sing a hymn to the Virgin Mary that he remembered from his childhood, when he had been a good boy with a pure heart. He sang with all his heart and soul, and the winds carried his song away, not up to heaven, but down to earth. The shepherds in the mountains heard it, and they felt happy and full of goodness.

Twardowski kept on singing as he was carried higher and higher, and people everywhere on earth heard him. Finally his voice gave out and he realized he was all alone. The devil had disappeared. He heard a voice coming from the clouds, like thunder: "You must stay here until Judgment Day!"

And so he is still hanging there, floating silently. Some old folks, remembering those tales of long ago, point to the moon when it is full and shining. "Look at that dark spot there," they say. "That is Pan Twardowski, sitting and resting on the moon."

JURATA, THE BALTIC QUEEN

This is one of the more important legends from the northernmost edge of Poland, in the area covering Pomerania and the Kaszubian Lake District. It is often used to explain the presence of beautiful chunks of amber that still turn up on the beaches of northern Poland.

*L*ong, long ago the Baltic Sea was ruled by a beautiful queen named Jurata. She had long hair and sea green eyes. She lived in a palace under the sea made of amber and gold, with windows that sparkled like diamonds and fish scales on the roof.

Over the Baltic roamed Perkun, old Slavic god of thunder and lightning. He had fallen in love with Jurata and decided that her home must never be disturbed by storms. So he refrained from sending his bolts of lightning and rolling thunder into the Baltic. It was almost always calm.

Jurata was a kind ruler. She made many laws protecting the sea and all within it. She did not allow anyone to catch too many fish or sea creatures, so they would always be plentiful. Jurata loved to eat flounder, but she did not allow anyone, even herself, to eat too many flounder. She tried to protect them from being caught.

On the Baltic coast lived a young human fisherman. He was very handsome and bold. He had little common sense. He had heard about Jurata and her laws, but he paid no attention. He set traps and lines and caught many fish. Thinking he could get away with all this catching of fish, he began to sell his catches in areas far away from the sea. Because he caught so many, especially flounder, that people liked to eat, he was able to sell his catches for a lot of money. He bought fine clothes and started to spend his money on drinking and making merry.

Jurata found out about the fisherman's excessive fishing and got very angry. She determined to punish him. She made a plan for the next time he came out to fish. She would swim close to him, catch hold of his leg, and pull him down deep into the Baltic, where he would drown.

But when she went off to carry out her plan and had her first glimpse of the fisherman, she forgot all she had decided to do. The fisherman was so handsome. She watched closely as he set his lines and traps, and the more she watched him, the more she fell in love with him. She decided to swim up to him and show her face.

When the fisherman saw her, he was struck by her beauty, as much as she had been struck by his good looks. He began to watch her as she swam close to him each evening. Every evening she came and every evening he was there to watch for her. He forgot about making merry with his friends. The more Jurata saw the young fisherman, the more she realized she could not harm him. The more the fisherman saw Jurata, the more he wanted her as his wife.

They met so many evenings that soon Perkun began to notice. He watched closely as Jurata and the fisherman exchanged loving looks.

"She has fallen in love with a human," said Perkun. "That is not allowed." He became so angry he began to build up a storm. He flashed his lightning and hurled his thunder, called up the winds, and soon they came. The Baltic Sea was churning and turning as it never had before. The storm was so fierce that it destroyed Jurata's palace and everything around it.

She was never seen again, nor was the young fisherman.

From that time, the pieces of Jurata's amber palace keep appearing from time to time on the beaches along the Baltic Sea. And some people living along the coast say they still hear the calls of Jurata and the fisherman, for each is still looking for the other.

JANOSIK

This character, similar to Robin Hood, is known throughout Poland and Slovakia and even parts of the Czech Republic. There are so many legends about him it is almost impossible to determine from which cultural group they originate. He became a very important folk hero in the late nineteenth century, when these peoples were trying to fight oppression by outsiders. There are numerous films and even a television series about his deeds. Some believe that all the legends were based on the deeds of one actual person, born in Slovakia in the late eighteenth century. But that person lived and operated as a thief for only about two years. It is much more likely that the legends are based on several persons, and that the tales were embellished to create wonder and interest.

anosik was born to a family living in the Tatra Mountains. When he was still a young child, he was given three magical gifts: a shirt, a belt, and a carved wooden ciupaga, a hatchet of the type used in the mountains. Because of these gifts, he could move from one place to another faster than the swiftest horse. Arrows that landed on him could not harm him. If he did happen to get a wound because he did not have his protection with him, he had magic herbs that he could smear on his skin, and the wound would disappear.

He loved to surprise some rich nobleman or magnate passing by on one of the paths that crossed the Tatras. He would steal their jewels and coins, and sometimes even their rich clothing. Then he would distribute his booty to poor families who were unable to pay their taxes, or to a bride who had no dowry and could not get married, or to starving beggars. He kept this up for many years.

His sweetheart was an innkeeper's daughter, and Janosik would visit her as often as he could. Some say it was she who betrayed Janosik when, one day, a police captain came to the inn. He was even more handsome than Janosik. The daughter fell in love with the captain, forgetting all about Janosik and the good he had brought to the poor families all around them. She hid his magic shirt, belt, and hatchet, and Janosik was captured.

Others say it was the innkeeper himself who betrayed Janosik. Still another legend says that one morning when he got out of bed, Janosik slipped on a handful of peas that had fallen (or been spread) on the floor, and before he could get to his magic shirt, belt, and hatchet, he was captured. He was sentenced to death, but was never forgotten.

MORSKIE OKO
(THE EYE OF THE SEA)

This ancient legend is set in the southeast corner of Poland, where it borders Slovakia and Ukraine. Not far away is Hungary. Many versions of the story refer to the foreigner as a Hungarian. It is difficult to imagine that there was once flat land here before the Carpathian Mountains rose up, but it is likely the land was rich and fertile. Villagers in this area tell this story as though it were true, at least in its basic outlines.

*J*n that place where the Carpathian Mountains are steep and surrounded by sharp cliffs, there were in times past fertile fields, pastures, and thick forests. There on the Polish border lived a powerful gentleman by the name of Morski. Morski means sea, and Pan Morski was very proud of this name.

On the other side of the border lived a young and handsome prince. His lands were good, but not as rich as those of Pan Morski. There was only a small strip of land between them. But this piece of land separated two very different peoples.

Pan Morski had a beautiful daughter. The neighboring prince saw her one day and fell in love with her the moment he first set eyes on her. He begged Pan Morski to give him the hand of his beautiful daughter in marriage. Pan Morski swore he would never allow this. He would rather have her marry the devil than marry a foreigner such as that prince.

Pan Morski was suddenly called away to fight for the Polish king, far away from his home area. He put his daughter in a convent and warned her to stay away from that foreign prince. He wanted her to marry someone from among their own people.

"I put a curse on you if you disobey me," he said to her before he left.

The lovely princess grew bored. The young prince continued to court her. He sent her lovely beads, ribbons, and jewels. He also sent an old fortuneteller, who predicted that she would become a great lady and live in a great palace with golden rooms. The princess made up her mind to defy her father and escape from the convent.

One night the prince came to the convent, dressed as a monk and accompanied by his sorcerers, dressed as beggars. The prince asked for alms for himself and his companions.

The nuns let him in past the gate. Immediately the sorcerers threw magic herbs in all directions. Everyone in the convent fell fast asleep, including the princess.

The prince fled with the sleeping girl and took her to his territory. He ordered his sorcerers to produce a huge palace of coral, studded with gold and gems. Magically, it appeared, and he put the sleeping princess inside.

She awoke and that day, and every day afterward, she spent her days dancing and wandering through the flowery meadows around the palace. In the evenings she was told pleasant stories, and musicians sang soft songs to her, so that she always had pleasant dreams. During the next seven years she had seven children, one each year. They grew up healthy and strong. No floods or hailstorms or illness came to trouble her or her children.

All that time Pan Morski was far away, fighting for the king. No word came back from him. Finally, people began to say he had been killed by the Tartars. His daughter heard this and started wearing black as a sign of mourning for her father. But in secret she smiled, for she thought that now her father's curse could not affect her. She claimed his lands.

One day, without warning, Pan Morski returned.

"Where is my daughter?" he shouted. His servants took him to the neighboring land, and there he saw the coral palace. His daughter came out to greet him, dressed in fine black clothes and wearing many jewels. She was accompanied by her children. Her father crossed himself, stamped his foot, and spat at the coral palace. It crumbled and disappeared in a cloud of dust.

"May your foreigner turn to stone, and all his possessions with him," shouted Pan Morski. When his daughter and her children came up to him on their knees, crying and asking for pity, he only got angrier and hurled these fateful words at them: "May you and your children melt in your own tears. You are no longer my daughter. They are not my grandchildren."

The fields, the meadows, the forests, the remains of the palace—everything turned into one giant rocky mountain. The prince, terrified, tried to escape as a monk, but he, too, was turned into stone. You can still see him in that spot in the Carpathians, where there is a huge rock shaped exactly like a monk in his long cloak.

The princess wept and called on her husband's sorcerers to help her. But they were not stronger than Pan Morski's curse. Each of the sorcerers picked up a child and started to run away, but the ground broke under them and they, too, turned to stone, dropping the children. The frightened children called to their mother. They each cried so much, small pools formed at their feet. Their mother came to them, weeping so many tears that a huge pool was formed around her. It was like a small sea because of the salt in her tears. People said she cried so much, one of her eyes actually fell into that sea. The princess threw her jewels into the sea and when nothing was left, she dissolved in her own tears and slipped into the water. Because she was still dressed in mourning black, the sea turned black. You can see how black it is, even today. It is called Morskie Oko, Eye of the Sea. People in that area say that if you go near the sea, you can hear the princess sighing and crying, because her father's curse has not been lifted and the princess's soul still does not have peace.

SOBOTNIA MOUNTAIN
or THE SEARCH FOR THE
WATER OF LIFE

Sobotnia means "Saturday," but we have not translated it here, because the name is so well known in the original. This mountain was sacred to the Slezan people, a pre-Christian tribe that lived in Lower Silesia. It was often the site of their rites. The verse toward the end is also a well-known folk song.

A widow had three sons, whom she dearly loved. Each of the sons had a different profession. The oldest was an organist in the parish church. He was clever and learned, for he could read books. He had even composed some hymns. Therefore he was much honored by the priest and his assistant.

The second son, the middle one, was a very noble knight. He roamed about and served different members of the nobility with distinction. He would listen carefully to people who talked about things he had not heard of before or learned about when he was still at home. He always remembered what he heard. This gave him much knowledge that others did not have, and it made him a very sought-after knight.

The youngest son stayed at home to help his mother. He worked the soil with a sweating brow, just as his father had done many years before. He was an innocent young man and sincerely believed anything and everything that was told to him, even though it might just be fanciful talk.

The three brothers loved their mother very much. Every day they tried to bring only joy and good things to her as she grew older. When one day she told them she felt ill, they gathered around her. She began to groan and moan in pain. The brothers could hardly stand it, and finally the organist told his two younger brothers to go and look for the Wise Woman who lived on the other side of the hill. She might have some herbs to ease their mother's pain.

The two went off and found the Wise Woman and asked her to return with them. When they got back, they met the organist at the door and asked if their mother was better, for they could no longer hear her groaning.

"I think she is better," he answered. "She is asleep and seems to have no more pain." But when the Wise Woman looked at their mother, she said she was not sleeping, but dead. The brothers began to weep and wail. Their grief was so terrible that the Wise Woman was filled with pity.

"If you want to bring your mother to life again, so she can spend a few more years with you, I can tell you what to do, but it is very dangerous. You will have to risk your own lives."

"Tell us," begged the brothers. "We will do whatever it takes."

"Beyond three rivers and three forests you will come to Sobotnia Mountain. If you go to the top, there you will find a talking tree. On it sits a hawk. Below that tree is a spring, and out of it flows the water of life. You can heal anyone who is sprinkled with this water. It will take you seven days to get there and back. When you get to the mountain, you must go straight up. Don't look to the right or to the left, no matter what you see or hear. Above all, don't look back, for you will be turned into a stone."

After the Wise Woman finished explaining, she left. The three brothers argued about who should go. Finally the knight said, "I'm used to traveling and facing death, so I should go. Wait a week and you will see; I'll return."

The other two brothers waited and waited and waited, but their brother did not come back. The organist then said, "I have a better head than you. I can even talk Latin. I will be a match for anything." And off he went.

The youngest brother waited and waited, but neither of his two brothers returned. So he set off, taking a loaf of bread and a scythe. He walked for three days and got to the foot of Sobotnia Mountain. When he looked up, he saw the summit hidden in the clouds. There was a path straight up, covered with slippery stones and many kinds of poisonous plants. There were other easier paths going off to the right or left, but he did not take them. He went straight up.

"Where are you going? That's the wrong way!" shouted a voice. He almost looked around, but remembered the Wise Woman's warning and just kept on going. Suddenly a man appeared in one of the paths at his right.

"Where are you going?" asked the man.

"To the top of the mountain."

"Why?"

"To look for the water of life."

"Come with me, then. That's why I'm climbing. And this path is easier."

"Take whichever path you want," said the youngest brother. "I'm going straight up on this one." And he continued on until he heard the barking of many dogs that seemed to be following him. He did not turn around. He saw he was close to the summit. A strong wind blew up. The trees began to give off sparks, as though they were filled with lightning. Suddenly he was brought up short because in front of him was a huge steep wall of rock. There was an opening in the rock, but it was guarded by a dragon with seven heads. The dragon was sleeping.

The youngest brother tried to sneak past the dragon, but it awoke and began to attack him. He took out his scythe and cut off its heads, one by one. Then he entered the opening in the rock, and soon he was in a beautiful garden, with trees that had silvery leaves and flowers shining like jewels. He heard nightingales singing, and in a clearing saw ten lovely girls dancing to the music. They beckoned to him, but he continued straight on. At last he came to a shining door, and when he opened it, there was the magic tree, with its silvery leaves and a spring gushing out of its roots. On the top of the tree was a golden hawk. At the sight of the peasant, the hawk spread its wings and flew off.

The peasant brother knelt down and drank some of the water. Immediately he felt refreshed, and all the cuts and bruises he had gotten during his climb disappeared. He felt like a new person. Suddenly he saw the hawk returning, carrying in its claws a golden jug. The hawk sang out:

> Take the golden jug, young man.
> Fill it in the fountain below.
> Break a branch off, if you can.
> Shake it well, as down you go.
> Dip it in the water, spray it,
> All along the way you walk.
> On your mother's bosom lay it;
> She will rise and she will talk.

The peasant took the golden jug and filled it with water. He broke a small branch off the tree and started to walk down. At every step he sprinkled the water over the stones, and out of them came men and women who then accompanied him on his downward journey. The farther he went, the more there were. All who had attempted to climb Sobotnia Mountain and had been turned to stone were now brought back to life: women, men, children, rich, and poor. Toward the bottom his two brothers, the organist and the knight, were restored to him.

All followed him, and after three days they reached his home. He sprinkled the water on his mother, and she opened her eyes and spoke to him. Everyone was excited and happy. In place of the small village, a big town grew up. In the middle of it the people built a beautiful home for the youngest son and his family. He married and lived many years, ruling over the grateful people he had restored with the water of life.

PART 4

Animal Tales

THE RIGHTEOUS RABBIT

There was once a good man named Matt who was poor, but honest in his simple way. One day he went to the forest to collect dead pieces of wood and twigs. He had gathered some in a heap, when he suddenly heard moaning from a spot nearby. It sounded as though someone was begging for mercy. Full of fear, he hesitated. Should he go, or stay and find out what it was? He decided to see if he could help. He approached the place cautiously. There he saw a bear, pinned down by a huge pine tree that had fallen on it.

"Have pity on me," growled the bear softly. "Lift up the tree and set me free."

Matt felt sorry for the bear. He set to work and found two tree trunks that had fallen. Pushing with all his might, he finally wedged the two trunks under the pine tree. The sweat poured off him, but at last he managed to free the bear. Tired and satisfied, he went home.

A few months passed. Matt had forgotten his generous act. Once again he went to the forest to get kindling. Suddenly, standing before him was that same bear he had set free a few months ago.

"Was it you who saved my life?" growled the bear.

"It was," answered Matt. "How have you been since then?"

"Well, you see, my friend, I should like to give you a reward. I am uneasy because I feel indebted to you for what you did."

"You want to give me a reward? I only did what many would have done," replied Matt.

"That's just it," said the bear. "I have this awkward feeling in the pit of my stomach that I must reward you by eating you. For as you know, in this world everyone repays good with evil, kindness with ingratitude. There is no other way. To follow the way of the world and get rid of this feeling, I must eat you."

"That is just a saying. Only evil persons talk like that. There is still much good in the world," insisted Matt.

The bear just laughed and said, "You are a foolish fellow. You obviously have not seen much of the world. But listen, if you can find someone who will agree with you, I will let you go."

"I will find someone," answered Matt, and he set off. Soon he met a peasant. "Friend, settle an argument between me and the bear," begged Matt. He told the peasant the whole story of the rescue. The peasant listened and then leaned over and whispered in Matt's ear.

"How much will you pay me if I agree with you? Otherwise, I'll have to agree with the bear."

"You see, I told you," said the bear.

Matt went along further until he met an ox. He told the ox his story and asked it to be the judge.

"Do I seem so stupid?" asked the ox. "You or some other human would slaughter me just as easily as that bear would eat you. Why should I worry myself about justice for you when there is none for me?" The ox bellowed, flipped its tail, and walked away.

Suddenly Matt heard a swallow up in a tree, chirping at him: "That judge was too big, Matt. And one too small will also not be good."

Just then Matt saw a ram. That seemed a good size: not too big and not too small. He went to the ram and asked his opinion.

The ram bleated, "I don't know about things like justice. If you want a good judge, go to the dog who guards our flock. Maybe you can even join us and always be told where to go and what to do. Then you don't have to worry about justice."

The bear heard that and was exultant. "Let's get on with it. Surely you can see that all agree with me. I need to repay good with evil. I need to eat you right now!"

"That ram was just a dumb follower of his flock. But it reminded me of someone I should consult: the dog. That is one creature who is always loyal and grateful."

Matt went to the dog and once again recited his tale. The dog listened and then barked his answer: "Last night some thieves tried to get in and rob and kill my master. I warned him with my barking and saved his life. Did he reward me? No, he kicked me and told me to be quiet so he could sleep."

"I was a fool to listen to that swallow," thought Matt. "Big or small, size has nothing to do with justice. Perhaps the horse will be fair. He's always ready to serve."

The horse came and listened to Matt, but then whinnied sadly, "I work hard for my master. I carry him, plow his fields and fertilize them, pull his wagon, and do many other tasks. And for all that he often beats me with a whip or pokes me with his spurs. Sometimes he does not give me anything to eat."

"Dear God," thought Matt. "Maybe goodness has disappeared from the world." He tried asking the fox, but the fox just told the bear to go ahead and eat. He went to the wolf, and the wolf suggested the bear might like to share Matt with him.

"That is definitely the final answer," said the bear.

But Matt got him to agree to just one more attempt at finding a judge who agreed with him. Once again, the swallow appeared. "Look for a creature that does no harm to anyone and yet has to hide from all. You'll find it under the bushes there."

Matt looked, and there was a rabbit. For the last time he repeated his story. The rabbit answered him softly, "I agree. Gratitude is hard to find because it comes from earthly creatures. But justice comes from God. If we go back to the place where this all started, maybe we can see some plan for justice."

They went to the edge of the forest and found the spot where the huge pine tree had fallen. It was still there, and the wedged logs were still holding it up off the ground.

"Now show me how Matt found you," said the rabbit to the bear. As soon as the bear was in place, the rabbit said, "Quick, Matt, pull out the wedged logs." Matt did, and the pine tree fell once again on the bear, pinning him down.

"Now everything is as it was before," said the rabbit. "Neither of you has to worry about gratitude. Justice has fallen on all." He turned to Matt. "Go home and give thanks that your life was spared. Try to keep gratitude and justice in your heart, even though you might be the last one on earth to believe in them."

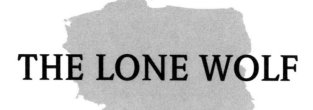

THE LONE WOLF

This is often called "The Wolf Goes in Search of Breakfast" in Polish.

*T*here was once a wolf who lived alone, instead of with a pack. Because of this, he also had to hunt alone, which meant he often went hungry. One night he dreamed of a delicious meal, all spread out before him. When he woke up, he was sure the dream was a sign he would soon eat well.

He had gone only a few paces when he saw ahead of him a mother goat and her two kids. Going up to her he said, "Nothing can help you now. I have a hunger such as I have never had. First I will eat your kids, and then you."

The mother goat bowed her head and acted as though she agreed. But first she asked the wolf if he would be kind enough to let them go to a nearby shrine and say a prayer before they died. The wolf agreed and followed behind them to make sure they would not escape.

When they got to the shrine, the goat and her kids began to bleat as loudly as they could. A shepherd nearby heard them and sent his dog to see what was causing all the noise. The dog was big and strong and trained to ward off wolves. He chased the wolf away from the mother goat and her kids.

The wolf was frustrated that such a delicious meal had escaped him. But just then he saw a mother pig and her nine piglets standing by the side of the road. He walked up to them and said, "Nothing can help you now. I have a hunger such as I have never had. I am going to eat you and your nine little piglets."

"Well, if it isn't now, it would be later," sighed the mother pig. "My master will soon butcher me in any case. But before you eat me and my children, please allow me one last favor. I want them to be baptized before they die."

The wolf agreed and followed her to a river, where a stream of water fell over a mill wheel. The mother pig told the wolf that the one who would baptize them was on the other side of the river, just above the place where the mill was situated. She put a long plank across the river and started across. The wolf followed along after her, balancing as best he could on the plank. Suddenly the mother pig jumped off, and the plank flew up at her end; the wolf lost his balance and tumbled into the water. He was carried right over the mill wheel and was caught in the paddles. The mother pig and her piglets quickly ran away.

By the time the wolf got out of the water and shook himself, there was no sign of them. He scolded himself for being so stupid. But not long after that, he met a rooster. He thought that the goat and kids, the pig and piglets, would have made a finer meal, but a rooster was good enough for now.

"Nothing can help you now," he said to the rooster. "I have a hunger such as I have never had. I will gobble you up before anyone can come to your rescue."

The rooster begged the wolf to let him crow one last time. But the wolf was now suspicious. "If I let you do that, you are certain to escape in some way."

"Hold my tail in your mouth while I crow, and then I won't be able to get away," said the rooster. So the wolf seized the rooster's tail between his jaws.

The rooster stretched his neck, flapped his wings, and crowed as loudly as he could: "Kee-kee-ree-kee!" (He was a Polish rooster, you know, and that's how they crow in Polish.) As the rooster crowed, one of his tail feathers came loose and stuck in the wolf's throat, and another feather floated up to his nose. It made the wolf sneeze so hard that he had to let go of the rooster. The rooster flew into a tree.

"How stupid I am," thought the wolf. He was sure he would have to go without food. But just then he met a fat goose. "Nothing can help you now," he shouted at the goose. "I have a hunger such as I have never had before. I will gobble you up now."

The goose agreed that she could not get away from the wolf, but she begged him to allow her to wash in the pond before he ate her.

"No," said the wolf, "for you will surely trick me."

"But can't you see, I have not been able to get to the pond for six days. I am filthy. Surely you do not want to eat all this dirt. You can hold me by the tail while I am washing myself."

Finally the wolf agreed, because he could see that the goose was very dirty. They went to the side of the pond, and while the wolf held on to her with his paws, the goose washed the front part of her body. Then she asked the wolf to let her go a bit deeper into the water, so that she could wash the other half. The moment they reached the deeper water, the goose took a steep dive, and she only came up when she was on the other side of the pond. She cackled and swam off before the wolf could reach her.

Tired and hungrier than he had ever been, the wolf limped along. He perked up when he saw a young mare with her foal standing in a field by the side of the road. "Nothing can help you now. I have a hunger such as I have never had before. I will eat you and your foal."

"You have no authority to do so," said the mare with a snobbish look. "I carry a letter that forbids anyone to touch me or my foal. Here, if you don't believe me, look under my hoof. That's where I keep it hidden." The mare lifted her right hoof, and while the wolf looked at it closely to discover what might be written there, the mare brought her hoof down on his head with such a bang he saw stars. The mare and her foal galloped off before he came to his senses.

The next animal the wolf met was a ram. He repeated his threat. But the ram seemed not at all upset by it.

"I am old, and it is time for me to die. Why don't you go down there at the bottom of the hill and hold your jaws wide open. I will come running down the hill and jump right in them."

This sounded like a fine plan to the wolf. He stood there, waiting, with his jaws wide open. The ram came down the hill with much speed, and with his horns held down in front of him. He butted the wolf so hard he turned somersaults and almost landed in a nearby lake. Before he could recover, the ram was gone.

"I can't believe I have been so stupid, so many times," said the wolf. He walked sadly back to the forest. "It is all my own fault. I should let someone cut off my tail to punish me."

A woodcutter was standing nearby, and with his axe he chopped off the end of the wolf's tail. The wolf went yowling through the forest, saying, "Wouldn't you know that would be the one wish to be granted!"

It is never wise to believe in dreams that seem too good to be true.

Cecylia Slapek, Cecylia Korban, and Janina Oleszek telling traditional stories at the Storyteller Museum during the Festival of Polish Oral Tradition

Traditional storyteller Cecylia Slapek telling the tale of Bald Montagne in her house in the Swietokrzyski Mountains

Traditional house in Suwalskie area

Highlander from Beskidy during Sabalowe Bajania Festival

Folk sculptures by Jan Bernasiewicz, in Tokarnia Open Air Muzeum

Photo by Michał Malinowski

Photo by Krzysztof Haladyna

Typical jump in folk dancing in Podhale

**Jan Kubik and his band of
folk musicians from
Kroscienko in Pieniny
Mountains**

**Jozef Piton, one of the most popular
contemporary-traditional storytellers
in the Tatra Mountains**

**Group of traditional singers
from Kurpie region**

View of Goloborze, on the Lysiec or Lysa Gora (Bald Mountain), from Swietokrzyski Mountain, the place of the mythological Sabbath of Witches

Traditional mountain food eaten during Sabalowe Bajania Festival

Traditional wooden house in Ostrow Mazowiecka

**Remek Hanaj and
Agata Hanaj playing
the hurdy-gurdy**

Typical Easter decoration

**Janina Mackiewicz,
traditional storyteller and
singer from the Suwalskie
area, in her house**

Michał Malinowski performing during storytelling workshop in the public library in Wegrow, Mazovia

View of front of Dom Ludowy during Sabalowe Bajania Festival, the most popular festival of traditional storytelling, singing, and music, held annually in Bukowina Tatrzanska in August

Traditional harvest holiday and Dozynki festival in Stanislawow, Kolbielskie area

Traditional costumes of Koleda, during which people dress up and go from house to house after Christmas, in Bukowina Tatrzanska

Traditional trumpet player from Krakowskie area

Piotr Makowski, traditional storyteller and folk singer from Mladz, Kolbielskie, in his house

Jozef Budz, traditional storyteller from Murzasichle in the Tatra Mountains

Interior of a house in the Krakowskie area, with the characteristic blue walls

THE CAT AND THE FOX

*O*ne day a cat met a fox. The fox wanted the cat to walk with him a while, so the cat agreed.

"I have seven kinds of wisdom," boasted the fox. "How many kinds do you have?"

"Well," answered the cat, "I have nine lives, but I have only one kind of wisdom. But I think it is a good piece of wisdom. It has served me well so far."

"And what is that one piece of wisdom?" asked the fox disdainfully.

"It is that I can think very quickly," answered the cat.

Soon after that they saw in the distance a group of hunters, leading their dogs on leashes. The fox noticed them first. "Let's run," he shouted. "I don't like hunters, with or without dogs."

"You claim to have so much wisdom," answered the cat, not moving. "I don't see hunters with dogs. I see farmers leading calves to the market." He convinced the fox he was right and that they should not run away.

As soon as the hunters saw the fox, they unleashed their dogs, and the dogs followed the scent of the fox very easily. They surrounded the fox so it could not get away. Soon the hunters would be there with their guns. The cat, meanwhile, scampered up a nearby tree, shouting at the fox, "You said you had seven kinds of wisdom, but I think I did better with my one kind."

THE FOX AND THE FISHERMAN

This tale is especially popular in the northern parts of Poland, in Warmia and the Masurian and Kaszubian Lake Districts.

One winter day fox got very hungry. He looked around in the snow to see if he could find food, but the snow was too deep. He was lazy and did not want to move through the heavy snow—it took so much effort. He decided to see if he could get food by playing a trick on someone. When he saw a farmer sitting under a pine tree, next to his cart, the fox began to sing to himself, "Hey, good buddy, my buddy, I will trick you, I will trick you."

This farmer, like so many of the farmers in the region, was also a fisherman. In winter he would chop a hole in the ice and fish. Every day he brought home a huge load of fish. That day he had been fishing and had sat down to rest a while before continuing on home. After he had rested he went back to the road, and there was the fox, lying down in the middle of the road as if dead.

The farmer sang softly to himself, "Foxy, my dear foxy, today I will catch you." Without checking carefully, he picked up the fox and put him in the cart on top of the fish. All the way home he dreamed of the fine fur he would get from the fox. Maybe he would have enough to make a muffler for his wife and a cap for himself.

As the farmer walked along pulling the cart, the fox was silently throwing out the fish, one by one, into the gully at the side of the road. As he was throwing out the fish, he sang softly to himself, "Hey, good buddy, my buddy, I am tricking you, I am tricking you." As soon as the cart was empty, the fox slipped out and went to collect the fish.

The fox went to put his fish in a secret hole in the middle of the forest. Who should see him but a jealous wolf. The wolf ran up to the fox and ordered him to tell what he had put in the hole. The fox would not tell at first, but then the wolf began to threaten him. At this, the fox said to himself, "Wolfie, good buddy, my wolfie, I will trick you, I'll trick you."

But aloud he said to the wolf, "Oh, I just put a bunch of fish I caught into that secret hole. I caught them by putting my tail down the ice hole that the farmer made so conveniently. The fish bite at it as though it is bait, and I just swing them out."

The wolf thought this was a fine idea and couldn't wait to try it. He set off for the lake, singing to himself, "Fishies, dear fishies, I will catch you, I'll catch you." When he got to the lake, he put his tail down into the hole and waited. That day the cold and the wind was terrific. Wolf was almost frozen, but he decided to wait it out until he caught at least a few fish.

Suddenly, who should come running to the hole but the farmer, being chased by his wife. She had refused to believe that he had caught a whole mess of fish but they had all somehow disappeared from his cart. She was chasing him back to the fishing hole so he could catch the fish they needed for their dinner.

As soon as they got near, the wolf tried to run away, but by this time his tail was frozen solid in the ice. He could not move. The farmer's wife and the farmer both attacked the wolf.

All the while, the fox watched this, and sang to himself, "Hey good buddy, my buddy, I tricked you. Wolfie, dear wolfie, I have tricked you."

MOTHER OWL AND THE HAWK

*O*ne day Mother Owl met Hawk. Now Hawk was always attacking baby birds in nests and eating them. Mother Owl was so afraid for her babies that she began to plead with Hawk, "Please don't gobble them up."

"How could I attack them when I wouldn't even recognize them?" asked Hawk innocently.

"It's very easy," replied Mother Owl. "My babies are the most beautiful in all the nests in all the forests."

Hawk promised he would not harm them and then flew away. He began to look for food. He passed many nests, and in many he saw beautiful, fluffy baby birds. Since they were all so beautiful, he passed them by, thinking they might be Mother Owl's babies. But one day he landed on the branch where Mother Owl had her nest. She was away, and her baby owls looked up with their big owl eyes. They looked so strange and ugly, Hawk was sure they could not belong to Mother Owl. He ate them on the spot.

Soon after that Mother Owl met Hawk again. She hooted and howled at him, "How could you do that, Brother Hawk? How could you eat my babies like that? You gave me a promise that you would not."

"I did not know they were yours. They had such big eyes and looked so strange and ugly. You told me you had the most beautiful babies in the whole forest. I stayed away from the beautiful baby birds."

Mother Owl went on her way sadly, thinking only how unappreciative of beauty the Hawk was. Why, her babies truly had had the most gorgeous eyes in the whole world. It is true what they say: One's own babies are always the most beautiful.

RABBIT STOPS COMPLAINING

*O*ne day Rabbit came to God and complained, "Why am I the only creature that has to run and hide from everyone? I even have to sleep with one eye always open. Yet no one seems to be afraid of me. It does not seem fair."

God answered Rabbit, "What you are saying is not true. I want you to go to the bank of the pond near you, and you will soon see that there is at least one creature that is afraid of you."

Rabbit hopped off to the pond. As he approached it, he heard the sound of croaking. Then, as he got right to the edge of the pond, he heard, "Ploom, ploom, ploom!" One by one, the frogs were jumping into the pond.

Rabbit sat at the edge and watched the circles spreading in the water, in all the spots where the frogs had jumped in. He was very happy that he had found at least one creature that was afraid of him.

PART 5

Magic Tales

THE FLOWER OF THE FERN

This tale is common throughout northern Poland, and similar versions are also found in Latvia and the Ukraine.

For a long time now, it has been known by elderly grandmothers, who tell many stories by the fire, that on midnight of Saint John's Eve, the fern flower comes into bloom. Saint John's Eve is June 23, usually the shortest night of the year.

The flower of the fern is hidden among steep hills, but those lucky enough to find it will have wealth all their lives. However, do not think it is easy to find the fern flower. After all, that is only one night in the year, and it is very short. Also, there is only one bloom among all the ferns in all the forests, and it is usually in the most difficult spot to get to, so hidden that one must have extraordinary luck to find it. Even if one is lucky enough to get near and catch a glimpse of it, it is still almost impossible to pluck it.

The flower is hard to recognize because at first it seems quite small and plain, with a stem barely long enough to break off. But it transforms itself into a gloriously beautiful flower with five shining gold leaves and shimmering blue petals. Many have tried to find the flower, but few have succeeded. One who did was Jacus.

As a youth, he was always filled with curiosity. He spent many hours questioning, listening, searching for answers to things that puzzled him. One day an old grandmother came to sit by his family's fire to share their meal. Jacus sat down next to her and began whittling on a stick of wood, trying to carve the likeness of the head of his dog, who sat by his side. The grandmother began to talk about the flower of the fern. Jacus dropped his stick and almost carved his fingers, he was so fascinated. She talked as though she had seen the flower with her own eyes, even though she had never picked it. When Jacus found out that the flower brought unending wealth, he determined that he was going to find it, come what may.

His home was next to a thick and extensive forest. He made up his mind that on the next Saint John's Eve he would look in that forest for the fern flower. If he did not find it on his first try, he would try again a year later. He waited patiently for Saint John's Eve to arrive. Finally, when the day came, while his siblings and friends went to play around the fire that was usually lit on that night, Jacus put on a clean shirt and went instead into the deep, dark forest.

He knew his way through the forest by daylight, but at night it looked so different. The trees looked enormous. Everywhere, nettles seemed to grab at him and sting him. He saw eyes shining among the trees and knew they belonged to animals, but he tried not to be frightened. But things seemed to conspire to make him turn back. If he landed in a piece of mud, it pulled at him as though to hold him fast. He saw clumps of grassy fronds sticking up through a swampy part and jumped from one clump to the next. When he looked back, the clumps looked just like human heads.

The path got easier after a bit, but he began to fear he would never find his way home again. Just as he was about to turn around and try to go back, he saw a huge clump of ferns in front of him. On one frond, close to the ground, there were five shining gold leaves, and in the middle, a flower that looked like a blue eye. It was spinning around like a pinwheel. His heart beat wildly as he reached out for it, but suddenly the flower faded away before his eyes and was nowhere to be seen. He heard what sounded like laughing, or perhaps frogs croaking. He fainted and fell to the ground.

When he woke up, he was back in his own house and his mother was leaning over him, crying. She and his father and the other children had searched for him and found him almost dead. He did not say a word about the reason he had gone into the forest. He simply made up his mind to try again the next year.

All year long he thought about it, but spoke of it to no one. When Saint John's Eve came again, once more he put on new clothes and set off for the forest, while the others were involved in the usual celebrations. This time the path seemed totally different. The trees did not appear as big, and they were not as close to each other. He came upon huge stones covered with moss. He passed many clumps of fern fronds, but none of them had a flower. The first clumps were as high as his ankles. The next were knee high. The following ones reached up to his waist. Then he came upon some that reached as high as his head. They seemed to be making a humming sound that was halfway between crying and laughing. When he stepped on one of the fronds that was bent over, it hissed at him. He grabbed it, and it shed blood. He felt as though he had been walking a long time instead of only one night, and still he found no flower. As he got ready to give up and turn around, he saw it.

It was the same flower, with the five leaves of shining gold, and the blue eye in the middle, twirling like a spinning top. This time he did not faint. He sat down on a nearby stone. He was so tired, he felt he had to rest. He fell asleep and dreamed the flower was laughing at him, asking him if he had had enough, and would stop pestering the ferns. One leaf seemed to get longer and longer and waved at him, as though it were a tongue sticking out at him.

When he awoke he was at the edge of the forest, near his village. He was still really tired. He could not remember if he had really seen the flower or if it was all a dream. But he determined to try it a third time. The third time is often lucky, he said to himself.

The next year he once again put on clean clothes and set off. This time the forest looked the way it usually did when he passed through it by day. No weird formations surrounded him. He walked along happily toward where he had found the ferns the time before. He found them again, but saw no flower. He knew it was now close to midnight. Desperately he looked this way and that—and there it was: the five golden leaves with the blue eye in the middle. He reached for it, and it burned his hand as though it were on fire, but Jacus did not drop the flower. The flower grew so bright, he had to close his eyes. He carefully placed the flower under his jacket, on his left side just above his heart.

Then a voice came from the flower, "You have got me! But just remember, the one who has me can have everything he desires, but he may not share it. The moment he does, he will lose all."

Jacus did not pay attention to what the flower was saying. He was thrilled to have plucked the flower successfully. He felt it clinging to his body as though it were sending roots right through his heart. He turned around and started to walk back to the village. The path was now shining. The flowers seemed to bow down as he passed. He began to feel tired and thought it would be nice to have a horse and carriage. The moment he had the thought, a carriage with six white horses appeared before him, accompanied by a coachman and liveried servants. He got into the carriage and began to think of the beautiful house he could provide for his family. No sooner had he had this thought, when a large castle appeared on the road ahead. He drove up to it, and there were more servants to wait on him—even a butler. He went into the castle and saw that every room was filled with beautiful things. He sat down at a table and wished for fine food, and it all appeared. Anything he thought of or wished for, there it was. He ate and ate and ate, and then went to sleep under silken coverlets.

The next morning he stepped outside into the garden behind his palace. On one side it was full of fruit trees, and on the other, a lovely wooded area. Through it all ran a silvery river. But the more he looked, the more he could not recognize anything. This was nowhere near his home. None of the people he saw passing by looked familiar. Then he remembered what the flower had said when he had plucked it: "The one who has me can have anything he desires, but he may not share it. If he does, he will lose all."

Jacus was having too much fun. He forgot about his family for the moment. He discovered a vault in the castle in which he found gold and jewels. After he had enjoyed looking at it for a time, he began to think how nice it would be if he could share some of it with his family. But every time he thought of doing it, he would recall the words of the flower, and he was not willing to give up his wealth. He decided they could look for the flower and find their own wealth. He lived a life of luxury and changed castles whenever he wanted. Sometimes he would ask for six brown horses instead of white ones.

In the end, he got tired of it. He thought of simple pleasures, such as the way his mother cooked things, or helping his father chop wood or make hay. He missed his home and family and all the people of his village. He felt brave enough one day to get in his carriage and ask the coachman to take him to his village. In a short time he was there, right in front of his old home. The village looked the same. Now that he was used to shining new things, everything there appeared old and worn.

Out of the house came an old woman, dressed in tattered clothes. She looked at the carriage in fear. Jacus stepped out, and at that moment his old dog came around the cottage and barked at him, not recognizing him.

"Mother, it is I, your son Jacus," he called.

"You are not my son. If he were alive, he would have come home to help us. We are all starving here. My son had a good heart. He would not have left us this way."

Jacus felt ashamed and reached in his pocket to touch the gold pieces he had there. As soon as he thought of taking them out, he felt a pressing on his heart, as though the fern flower covered it with a tight piece of armor. His heart hardened as though it were filled with stone. He got into his carriage and returned to his palace without once looking back.

But once he was back, his mother's words kept coming back to him. At the castle, he ordered an orchestra to come and play music, and couples to start dancing, while he watched and ate and drank. But they were all strangers. He felt sadder than ever. But the stone was still in his heart.

After another year, he could bear it no longer. He went back to his village. This time, his mother did not come out to greet him. When he asked where she was, his youngest brother said she was in her bed, very ill. His father was already dead, and they had almost nothing to eat. Once again Jacus fingered the gold in his pockets, and once again, when he made a move to take it out, the armor of the fern flower pressed against him and he could not bring himself to do it. It was as though the flower were telling him, "Your mother will die soon anyway and you have most of your life still ahead of you."

So again he returned to his castle. But this time only a few months passed before he began to regret his actions. His conscience pricked him more and more. He grew thin and unhealthy. He felt tortured and slept poorly. Finally, after one sleepless night he took a large amount of gold and set off for his old home, resolved to give up his rich life this time.

He arrived at the cottage, but no one was there. A beggar came by and asked what Jacus was doing there. He replied that he was looking for the family who had once lived in that cottage. The beggar told him no one lived there anymore. All had died of starvation. Even most of the villagers had died, for times had been very hard. When Jacus heard this, he felt his frozen heart melt. He felt he would die of shame. And as soon as he had had that thought, the earth opened up, and he disappeared, taking the fern flower with him. Some say it grew up again, but no one has seen it since.

THE GLASS MOUNTAIN

The motif of a castle on top of a glass mountain is very common in European tales, and Poland is no exception. The elements that make it distinctive here are the addition of the apple tree and the blood that brings the dead suitors back to life.

On top of a glass mountain there was a golden castle. In this castle lived an enchanted princess, cast under a spell that was to last for seven years. She was very beautiful and very rich and spent most of her time in a silver room hidden deep inside the castle. The cellars below her castle were filled with chests of precious jewels and gold. In front of the castle grew a tree bearing golden apples. This tree was protected by a fierce falcon. The falcon was really the witch who had put the spell on the princess; she had taken this disguise to protect the princess in her palace. If you were able to get to the top of the mountain, and past the falcon, to pick one of the apples from the tree, you would be allowed into the castle.

Many knights had tried to do this. They used their best horses, shod with fancy shoes, but still they failed to get to the top. Their bodies, still clad in heavy armor, lay strewn about the mountain.

One day, a few days before the seven years were up, a knight in golden armor came along to try. He knew that the princess and all her wealth would vanish the moment the seven years came to an end. The knight made it halfway up, and then calmly walked down again. On the second day, he almost reached the top. Suddenly, the falcon attacked him and his horse, pecking at their eyes so they could not see. They fell backward to their deaths.

A young scholar heard about all these attempts and decided to try his luck. He was tall and handsome and very clever. He knew he had to try a method different from that used by all the knights. First he went to the forest and killed a lynx. He took the sharp paws of the lynx and attached them to his hands and feet. When he got to the bottom of the glass mountain, he saw that it looked like a giant cemetery. He could hear the bones rattling in the armor of the dead knights.

The young man started climbing up the mountain, using the sharp claws to keep from sliding back down. He went up very quickly and was more than halfway up, when he stopped to rest a while. He was hungry and thirsty, but he had nothing to eat or drink. Just

---

The Glass Mountain

then the falcon flew down, thinking it could attack the young scholar and gouge out a bite of flesh. The falcon dug its claws into the young student, but in spite of his wounds, he grabbed hold of the falcon's legs and held on tight. When it flew up, he was carried along. He scratched at the falcon with the claws on his hands, and the falcon began to bleed. The drops of blood scattered far and wide over the mountain, falling on the dead knights. As soon as a drop of blood touched a knight, he sprang up alive. Soon, all of the knights were able to get up and walk away.

The scholar saw they were now flying over the apple tree. He clawed with all his might until the legs of the falcon came off, and it fell tumbling to the ground. The young scholar landed on one of the branches of the apple tree. Quickly he plucked an apple and cut it in half. He rubbed the peel against the places where the falcon had cut into his flesh. All of his wounds were healed. Then he picked a handful of apples and walked toward the palace. The golden gates opened wide, and he saw a beautiful courtyard with fountains and trees and flowers.

High up in the tower, the princess looked out from her window and saw him approach. She ran to greet him with open arms. They made plans for a wedding. But they never could go down from the mountain to live among ordinary folk, because the falcon had died before it could release the princess from her spell. People say they lived a long and happy life together, in the palace at the top of the glass mountain.

THE FOOL WHO SEARCHED FOR FEAR

This is another tale that is quite common in other parts of Europe. Here, the element of exaggeration makes it more humorous than other versions.

There were once two brothers named Paul and Saul. Paul always thought just what everyone else was thinking. He never came up with a new idea, but people thought he was smart because he always agreed with them, and they always agreed with him. Saul, on the other hand, was thought to be a dunce. Everyone called him a fool. If anyone talked about being afraid, Saul simply could not understand.

"What is this thing called Fear that you are talking about?" he would ask. "Does it hurt? What does it look like? Is it big or small? Does it have a tail? Does it have two eyes? Can you eat it?"

Paul got fed up with his brother's questions. One night he decided to teach him a lesson. Saul was supposed to go to the tavern for his father and bring back a bottle of vodka. Paul knew that Saul would pass through a graveyard on the way to the tavern and back, for it was the shortest path. Paul put on an old red dress he found in his mother's closet. He took a piece of coal, wrapped it in an old towel, and put it in his open mouth, so one side of the coal shone out from between his teeth. He truly looked like a monster. He waited on the path in the graveyard for Saul to pass by.

As soon as Saul saw Paul a little ways ahead, standing in the path, he called out, "Hey, you with the light in your mouth, get out of my way or else I will have to step on some of those muddy graves."

Paul began to moan and groan as weirdly as he could, but he did not move.

"Are you deaf?" shouted Saul. "Get out of the way or I'll smack you."

Paul spread his arms and waved them and wailed in a high voice, as though he were a ghost. Saul jumped on Paul and began to punch and kick him. Paul finally managed to spit out the coal and tell him who he was.

"Is it really you, Paul? I am sorry. Why is a clever fellow like you standing here in the graveyard with a dress on and a coal in your mouth?" Paul was so angry, he could not bring himself to answer. He limped home behind Saul.

When their father heard what had happened and saw the state his son Paul was in, he was even more furious. He took a whip and chased Saul, ready to give him a beating. But Saul climbed into the hayloft and slept there that night.

The next day the doctor had to be called, and this cost a lot of money. The father was now so angry he threw Saul out of the house and told him not to come back until he managed to find out what Fear was. Saul's mother begged her husband to give their son one more chance, but he refused. So poor Saul took his few belongings and a few coins his mother managed to give him, and set off to search for Fear.

A week later he came to a small town that was very busy and full of people, for it was market day. When he stopped at an inn to eat, everyone inside was laughing and joking and celebrating the good exchanges they had made in the market. One of the men noticed Saul and asked him who he was and where he was going.

"I'm Saul, but I don't know where I'm going because I am in search of Fear, and I don't know where to look." Everyone laughed at that.

However, the innkeeper stepped forward and said, "If that is what you are looking for, you can find it up in that castle on the hill. No one wants to live there because of the ghosts. It has been empty for a long time. I suggest you go up there and try to spend the night. I think you will find Fear, all right."

"I'm ready to try it. Just give me plenty to eat and drink, so I won't get hungry or bored. I'll pay you when I get back," said Saul.

Most of the men there tried to talk him out of it, saying he would surely end up dead, but the more they argued, the more Saul wanted to try it. They finally helped him to carry a load of firewood into the main castle hall, and the innkeeper's wife loaded him down with sausage, potatoes, and a bottle of vodka. They did not say "Good night," they said "Good-bye," for they were sure that Saul would be dead by morning.

Saul settled down for a long night in the castle. He pulled a table and chair up to the fireplace, set fire to a nice heap of logs, lit his pipe, and began to listen to the wind howling. You would have been frightened at the strange sound this made, but Saul thought it was just nice music. He set out his food and began to eat, when had he done that, he heard a ghostly voice in the chimney say, "I'm coming down."

"Right in the middle of my supper," complained Saul. "Well, come on down, then, I don't care."

There was a banging and rattling, and down the chimney came half of a man. It was just the part from the waist to the feet. Saul took hold of one of the feet and threw the half-man across the room. He sat down to eat, and once again came that ghostly voice from the chimney, "I am coming down."

"Go or come. If you are part of the Fear I'm supposed to be looking for, you can go to the devil," said Saul. Just then the top half of a man landed in the fireplace. He had a bushy beard, and his eyes rolled around like red marbles. Saul took hold of one of his arms and tossed him in the same direction he had tossed the bottom half. He waited to see if anything else would come down the chimney, but nothing did, so he sat down to eat.

Suddenly, standing behind his chair was a huge figure with blood red eyes that rolled and a bushy beard.

"What are you standing there for?" asked Saul. "If you want something to eat, sit down and I'll share with you. I don't like eating alone anyway." The figure sat down but did not begin to eat.

"Help yourself," insisted Saul. But the strange being did not reach out for any food, until Saul was ready to eat his last sausage.

"Forget it," said Saul. "You did not want it when I offered it to you, so go suck your thumb!" He popped the last sausage into his mouth.

"Are you not afraid of me?" groaned the strange figure. "Don't you know the meaning of Fear?"

"My smart brother keeps talking about this Fear, and my father chased me out of the house to go look for it, but where is it? Everyone talks about it as though it were real, but I have never seen it close enough to touch it. What is it, anyway?"

When Saul spoke those words, the figure burst into tears. "Thank you! You have saved me. I used to be the lord of this castle, and I ruled with an iron hand, mostly by striking terror into the hearts of my subjects. But a hundred years ago some demons put a spell on me and turned me into a creature who would cause most people to die as soon as they looked on me. I was ready to tear you to bits and eat you, but you stood up to me. Because in the end you did not give me food, you have set me free. For Fear feeds upon food, and if you do not feed it, it will gradually disappear."

"That's fine," said Saul. "But can you give me something to take back to my father so he will let me in the house again?"

"I will give you enough treasure to blind you and your father," answered the lord, now restored to his old form. "Come with me." He took Saul to a secret dungeon, and there they found gold and silver and jewels so shining that Saul was almost blinded by their glare. The lord told Saul he could take as much as he wanted.

"My brother Paul would know just what to take, but I am not as smart as he is. So I'll just take this big diamond," said Saul. He picked up a jewel as big as a goose egg and in the morning went back to the inn.

The innkeeper could hardly believe his eyes. "Didn't the ghost come out and scare you?" he asked. By now, Saul was a bit wiser than he had been before.

"Yes, the ghost came and scared me and beat me, but I just managed to escape. I know I promised to pay you, but I barely got away," said Saul. And all believed him, so he could set off for home with the diamond in his pocket. A few months later, many were surprised to find out that Saul had married a woman of the nobility. He became famous for the fine dinners he served, and many called him Saul the Wise. Now he seemed to think and act just the way everyone else thought and acted. But did he ever find Fear? Who knows?

MADEJ'S BED

This is still one of the most frequently told tales in the Holy Cross Mountains. It is one of a cycle told about Madej, the robber.

*O*nce there was a trader from Krakow who traveled from place to place. While he was passing through the mountains, he realized that he was lost. He knew this was the place where the wicked robber Madej preyed upon people and stole all their goods and money. Madej prowled about the forest, armed with a huge club made from a thick tree branch. Some said Madej was so cruel, he had killed his own father. Suddenly the trader heard wolves howling and was even more frightened, so he shouted for help. There appeared before him a forest devil.

"I will show you the way out, but when you get home, you must promise to give me the newest thing in your house when I come for it," said the devil. The trader agreed, and the devil made him sign a contract in blood.

When the trader returned to Krakow, he found that his wife had just given birth to a baby boy. The trader moved his family in hopes the devil would never find them. The boy grew up to be a clever young man. He could see that his father was always worried before he set off for trading. He pleaded with his father to tell him why he was always so anxious. At last, the trader told his son the secret. He described the forest where it had happened.

"Don't worry," the young man reassured his father. "I will know how to deal with it." Now the young son had been all set to go off and begin his studies as a priest, but as soon as his father had gone to do more trading, he determined to first settle with the devil. His mother gave him food, holy water, and a holy card with prayers. He started for the forest where his father had met the devil. He walked and walked until he came upon a small hut. Inside the hut was an old woman. The young man entered and asked her for a place to rest and a bite to eat.

The old woman was afraid. She gave him something to eat but then told him he must hide, because her son, Madej, would be home soon, and there was no telling what he would do. He might kill the young man on the spot.

The young man hid as best he could, but as soon as Madej returned, he smelled the presence of a stranger in his hut. He pulled the young man out from his hiding place and shouted, "What are you doing here?"

The young man answered truthfully, "I am on my way to look for the devil's cave that is supposed to be near here. I want to ask him to give back the contract my father was forced to sign in blood."

"Well, in that case," growled Madej, "perhaps you can find out what plans the devil has for me. I've been a wicked fellow, I know, and it would be good to prepare myself. If you promise to return here after you have found the devil's cave, and can tell me what the devil plans to do with me, I will let you return to your father's house."

The young man gave his word of honor he would do so. He set off for the area his father had described and found one entrance to a cave, but it was closed tight and could not be opened. He walked on and found a second entrance. There was a huge rock suspended over the entrance. The young man threw holy water at the rock and took out the holy picture his mother had given him. The gate opened and the rock did not fall. He entered and could hardly move forward, the smells were so bad. Suddenly he was surrounded by agitated devils, trying to chase him back out of the cave. They recognized that he was an innocent young man and did not belong there. The devil chief stepped forward and asked what he wanted.

"I have come for the contract you forced my father to sign," said the young man. "It was signed in blood, but it was innocent blood. You had no right to make him do it."

The devil did not want the young man to stay there. He could only cause trouble. So he agreed to give up the contract. He brought it out, and the young man was ready to leave with it, when he saw something in a corner. It looked like an iron bed, full of sharp knives sticking up all around. Beside the bed was a fierce fire. Over the fire was poised a hot cauldron of boiling tar, slanted forward so that drops of the hot tar dripped onto the bed, one by one.

"What is that?" asked the young man in surprise.

"That is waiting for the robber Madej," replied the devil. "We are sure his luck will not hold out much longer; he will soon be here."

The young man hurried away as fast as he could. He returned to Madej's house and told him what he had seen: the iron bed with the knives and the hot tar dripping slowly over it. Madej decided then and there that he must change his ways.

"If I repent my sins, do you think I can avoid that?" Madej asked.

"Yes, I am sure you can," answered the young man. "But you must truly be sorry and admit all of the evil you have done. After I have become a priest I will return, and then you must confess all your sins. In the meantime, you must try to do good to those you have harmed."

Madej stopped robbing people. He took his special club and planted it in the ground. It grew up into a beautiful apple tree and finally, after several years, it was covered with apples. Madej continued to do good wherever he could.

One day a bishop was riding by the forest in his carriage, with a retinue of servants and guards. He asked the carriage driver to halt, because he had suddenly smelled the most wonderful perfume. It seemed to surround his carriage. He looked all around, and in the distance saw a huge apple tree, covered with apples. Under it sat a very old man. It was Madej.

When Madej looked up, he cried, "It is you. You have come back!" For it was indeed the young man who had passed there many years ago and convinced Madej to change his life. They recognized each other and embraced. Madej said he wished to make his confession and be forgiven. He recited his sins, and as he voiced each one, an apple fell from the tree and turned into a dove, which flew away. Finally, when Madej said he had finished, there was still one apple hanging from the tree.

"Have you truly admitted to all of your sins?" asked the bishop. And Madej, with tears in his eyes, at last admitted that, long ago, he had killed his father. At that moment the last apple turned into a dove and flew away, and Madej slipped to the ground and died peacefully.

THE CROWN OF THE SNAKE KING

There are a number of versions of this tale, but in this one the male hero has the unusual name of Pearl, more often given to a female.

A long, long time ago in Poland, there lived a widow with her only son, who was called Pearl because of his pure heart and virtuous character. They were very poor. They ate the vegetables they grew or mushrooms and berries from the woods. They drank milk from their one cow. But they always shared what little they had with anyone who passed by.

One day, on his way home from gathering firewood in the forest, Pearl heard whimpering. He soon saw that it came from a small puppy, tied on a leash, that a cruel-looking man was pulling along.

"What are you going to do to that dog?" asked Pearl.

"I am taking him to the river to drown," answered the man. "He is no use to me."

"If you give him to me, I will take care of him," said Pearl.

The man gave the dog to Pearl and went off. But he did not take the dog to drown; he took it home to his mother.

"Oh, dear, we have so little to eat, and you bring another mouth to feed," she lamented. But Pearl said he would share his own food with the dog. The dog grew into a fine worker. It would retrieve animals that Jan hunted so that they often had meat to eat, such as wild hare or partridge.

The next year, Pearl brought home a kitten. Again his mother scolded him, but again Pearl insisted he would feed the kitten from his own food. It soon grew into a fine fat cat, and there were no more mice or rats coming near their storeroom.

In the third year, Pearl was walking by a field and saw that the reapers were cutting only around the edges of the field. When he asked them why, they replied that there was a fierce snake in the middle. They were afraid of being bitten by it, so they did not cut there.

Pearl was not afraid of any animal, and he offered to get rid of the snake for them. The reapers were delighted to accept. So Pearl cried, "Snake, snake, come to me and be mine." Out came a huge snake with beautiful marks on its shining body. It coiled itself around Pearl's neck, and he took it home.

Now his mother was really angry. "The dog and cat were fine because they have helped us. But what help can such a snake be, and what will it eat?" she cried.

"I will give it the milk I usually have for breakfast," said Pearl. "See how beautiful it is, and so gentle."

The snake would lie in the sun by day and at night slept next to Pearl in his bed. Every morning it drank milk from the cow. Curiously, the cow seemed to give more milk than before.

One day robbers tried to enter the house at night. The dog barked, the cat meowed, and the snake hissed so loudly that the robbers ran away.

Time passed. Pearl could see that the snake grew very unhappy. "Why are you looking so sad?" he asked. How surprised Pearl was when the snake answered him.

"I am the son of the king of the snakes. I once lived in a palace with my father. He has royal marks on his skin like no other snake. He wears a small crown on his head that has all the colors of the rainbow. There are no other snakes in all of Poland like him, and I would like to go back to him, but I do not think I can find my way alone."

"How did you get here?" asked Pearl.

"I was sunning myself one day, and a huge bird swooped down and picked me up and carried me off. After a long flight I managed to wiggle free, and I fell in the meadow where you found me. Please, Pearl, help me return to my father. Then you can ask him to give you the crown as a reward. It is a magic crown and will do whatever you ask."

Pearl agreed, and they set off. They crossed rivers and swamps. They passed through dense forests and up over high mountains. At last they came to a place that was filled with snakes—big and little, fat and thin, short and long. Pearl knew that they were now in the land of snakes. In the middle he saw a fine palace, overgrown with mistletoe. The king of the snakes lay in front, sunning himself. His shining body was covered with unusual marks. On his head sparkled the crown. It was small—no bigger than a large ring—but it was covered with jewels of many colors.

"What are you doing here?" hissed the snake king.

"I've brought back your son," answered Pearl.

The king was overjoyed. He asked immediately what reward he could give Pearl.

"I would like your crown," said Pearl.

"Are you sure? It will not bring you happiness. It would be better to ask for something else. It is impossible to buy love."

"I want only your crown," insisted Pearl.

"Very well then, take it. But I assure you, it will not bring you happiness. Some day you will come back and return it to me, for it is a crown that is very hard to bear." Saying that, the snake king handed Pearl the crown and slithered away.

Pearl returned to his home with the crown, and for a time all went well. He would ask for food, and a table would appear. He and his mother and the dog and cat lived a life of ease. But Pearl decided it was time for him to marry. Now that he was rich, he was sure he could ask for the hand of a princess.

He set off for the palace, dressed in his best clothes. But the princess, when she came near him, said, "You are nothing but a peasant boy, in spite of your fancy clothes. I can still smell the grease in your hair. Besides, I am already betrothed, and to a fine prince at that." Nevertheless, Pearl still wanted to marry her.

The king decided he had to get rid of Pearl somehow. He ordered him to level a mountain nearby, so it would be half as high. The earth that came off was to be used to fill in a swamp. Then he was to build a castle on the top of the flattened mountain. Perhaps if he could do that he would be worthy of the princess.

Pearl went to the mountain, took out the magic crown, and wished for it all to happen. Before you could blink your eyes, there was the castle on the flattened mountain. Again Pearl went to ask for the hand of the princess, and this time her father consented, because he dreamed of all the wealth the marriage would bring to him. The preparations for the wedding began.

Now the princess had no intention of marrying Pearl. She simply wanted to find out how he had done his magic. She pretended to flatter him and did everything to win his confidence. Finally, she asked him how he did his magic. Unsuspecting, Pearl told her the whole story, about the crown from the king of the snakes. He took it out of his pocket to show her.

That night the princess gave Pearl a fine feast and served it with much wine. Pearl fell sound asleep at the table. The princess slipped her hand in his pocket, took out the crown, and then wished that he would return to his home.

When Pearl woke up, he found himself once again in his modest home, with his mother, the dog, and the cat. He wept bitterly at his foolishness. But then he and the dog and the cat decided they must get the crown back and return it to the snake king.

They set out for the palace where the princess lived. They arrived at nightfall. The dog and the cat convinced Pearl to wait in the forest while they went ahead to see what the situation was like. The dog and the cat came to the moat surrounding the castle. The cat climbed on the dog's back, and they swam to the castle.

Suddenly they heard the sound of wedding music. It seemed to be coming from a small hole in the wall. Sure enough, out came a mouse bridegroom and bride, followed by some mouse musicians. The cat was ready to jump in and scatter the whole party, but the dog said, "Seize the bride and do not harm her. Touch no one else. Then, obey the commands I give."

The cat jumped on the bride and held her between his paws. The dog then told the other mice that she would be set free if they could find the crown and bring it to them.

The mouse bride squeaked, "I know the secrets of the house. I have seen the princess carry the crown with her all day long. She never puts it down. At night, she sleeps with it hidden under her tongue."

"Very well," said the dog to the mouse groom. "If you go and get the crown, we will let your bride free. But if you fail, the cat will crunch her up and eat her, whiskers and tail and all."

The mouse groom hurried off to the princess's room. She was sound asleep. With his whiskers, he tickled her under her chin. Her mouth flew open, and out popped the crown. The mouse groom ran and gave it to the dog, the cat released the mouse bride, and the wedding could continue.

The dog and the cat ran back to the moat, and the dog told the cat to hold on to his back once again and carry the crown in his mouth. The dog began to paddle, and when they were halfway across he called out to the cat, "Cat, are you still holding on to the crown?"

"Yes, I am," said the cat. But as soon as he opened his jaws the crown fell into the water. When they got to the other side, the dog discovered what had happened. He was obliged to take the blame. So he thought of another plan.

"Surely a fish has swallowed the crown. Cat, I will plunge into the water and chase the fishes, one by one, to the shore. You reach out and catch them. Open their bellies to see if the crown is inside." Before long, the shore was lined with fish.

"What is going on here?" cried the ruler of the fishes.

"We have lost the crown of the king of the snakes. It is the property of our master, and we must get it back. Until we do, we will chase the fish and open their bellies, for we are sure one of them swallowed it."

The ruler of the fishes called all the fish together. One by one, each was asked, "Did you swallow the crown?" Finally a young fish admitted he had swallowed it, thinking it was something good to eat. He spit it out on the shore, and the dog picked it up and took it back to Pearl.

Pearl went to the king and the princess and said, "You and your daughter have deceived me. She stole the crown from me. I want some justice, or I will order the crown to take revenge for me."

Frightened, the king said, "Choose what punishment the princess should have. We will see it is carried out."

Then Pearl remembered the words the snake king had said so long ago. "You must marry the prince to whom you are betrothed," he said to the princess. "I can level mountains and create palaces, but I cannot order someone to love me."

So the princess was married, and Pearl and the dog and the cat set off once more for the country of the snakes. When they got there, he put the crown on the head of the snake king. The snake king said to him, "I told you that neither this crown, nor any other, can bring true happiness. For happiness does not come from possessions or from being admired. It can come only from love, which you cannot buy. And even love, sooner or later, seems to disappear."

THE HATCHET OF JANOSIK

This is one of hundreds of tales that follow the Janosik cycle (see the Janosik legend in part 3). In the original Polish of A. J. Glinski, he uses the term "sword" rather than hatchet. Because he was known for creating literary versions of folk and fairy tales, it is likely that he wanted this to be compared to the sword in the stone mentioned in the King Arthur legends and changed the original from a hatchet to a sword. The word "hatchet" is used here as more in keeping with the Janosik legend.

On the shore of the Dunajec River, near to the place where Janosik's hatchet was buried in a stone, stood the manor house of a nobleman. He had three pretty daughters. The nobleman possessed few lands, but he did have one thing that gave him all the riches he needed. While he was still a young man, a falcon had passed over his land, carrying in its beak the seed of an apple from the Garden of Paradise. The falcon had accidentally dropped the seed, and there in the garden grew a wonderful tree. Its branches were soon covered with apples of gold. The falcon stayed by it, watching over it. Every morning at dawn, the nobleman would shake the tree and three apples fell down—only three.

While the nobleman and his wife lived, the three daughters behaved well, but as soon as their parents died and they became mistresses of the manor house and the tree, they grew proud and haughty. They became greedier and greedier. They spent the gold from the three apples on finery and never shared with the poor.

Soon young men came to see if one of them, at least, would marry. But the sisters were too proud. If a nobleman came, they would insist on a knight. If a knight came, they would insist on a duke. If a duke came, they would insist on a prince. And if a prince came, they would insist they could only marry the son of an emperor.

To get rid of the suitors, the three sisters thought of impossible tasks. They let it be known they would only marry someone who could move the mountain of Giewont to another spot; then drink up all the water in the Dunajec River; and finally, capture lightning in the palm of his hand. One after another, the suitors left, sighing because they could not have one of the sisters *and* the magic apple tree. Soon no more suitors arrived, because they all saw that it was hopeless.

Now in a valley nearby there lived a shepherd named Yendrik. He was as fast on his feet as a mountain goat. He heard of the three sisters and thought maybe they would prefer a shepherd. He went off to their manor house and said, "Look here. I would like to marry. Will one of you take me as a husband?"

How the sisters laughed. They had turned away noblemen, knights, and princes. And here was a shepherd thinking he could marry one of them. They each did think, secretly, that he was very handsome, but they reminded him of the difficult tasks he would have to perform: move Giewont Mountain, drink up all the water in the Dunajec River, and capture lightning in the palm of his hand.

"Of course," said Yendrik. "I know all about those. They should not be too difficult, with the special powers I have."

When the three sisters heard how confident Yendrik was, they felt they must devise a new test. They whispered to each other, and finally presented the new challenge to him: "You must draw the hatchet of Janosik out of the stone in which it is buried. Then with the hatchet you must cut down the apple tree in our garden. If you do that, whichever one of us you choose will be your wife."

Now each of the sisters was thinking secretly how handsome Yendrik was. He was better looking than all of their previous suitors. They were getting on in years, and now no one was coming to ask for their hands in marriage. The oldest sister went to Yendrik in secret and whispered to him, "I have read in a book that Janosik's hatchet is buried in a stone at a place called Eagle's Edge. Now remember, it was I who told you."

Yendrik then went to the second sister when the other two were not looking. He looked very sad as he told her that he truly wanted to marry, and he knew where Janosik's hatchet was, but he was not sure how to get it out.

The second sister replied in a whisper, "My father once told me that if the right young man climbed up to Eagle's Edge, keeping the Giewont Mountain on his right and Eagle's Edge on his left, he would soon come upon the stone. If he got to the stone early in the morning when it was wet with dew, it would grow soft for just the moment when the first rays of the sun hit it. Then one could pull out the hatchet. Now remember, it was I who told you this."

The third sister suspected something. She went to Janosik, late on the night before he was to set off on his task, and whispered to him, "When you are climbing up the valley, just before you get to the place called Eagle's Edge, you must call out 'Janosik' three times. If you hear an echo, you know you are near the hatchet, but if you hear no echo, you will not be successful. Now remember, it was I who told you."

Early the next morning, long before the sun was up, Yendrik set off, keeping Giewont Mountain on his right and Eagle's Edge on his left. When he came near to where the stone was supposed to be, he called loudly, "Janosik! Janosik! Janosik!" Back came the echo, rolling down from the mountaintop.

Scrambling quickly, so as to reach the stone before the sun came up, Jendrik arrived and felt the dew on all the stones. Many were so covered with moss, he could hardly recognize the one in which the hatchet of Janosik was buried. But at last he saw the handle sticking up. He grasped it and waited patiently for the sun's first rays to hit the rock. When they did, there was a flash like lightning, and Yendrik could pull out the hatchet as though it were coming out of butter. He walked back to the manor house and the three sisters.

When he entered the garden, they saw that he was carrying the hatchet. "Do you remember, it was I who helped you," they each cried at the same time. Yendrik said he did, but that first he must cut down the tree. He began to chop at it with the hatchet. The falcon kept screeching, but Yendrik continued to chop. There was a loud crack, and down fell the tree. The golden apples lay scattered like hail on the ground. Yendrik took his knapsack and filled it full of golden apples.

"Choose, choose, choose," cried the sisters impatiently.

"Which one?" asked Yendrik.

"Me, of course!" cried the eldest sister. "I told you where to find the hatchet."

"No, me!" yelled the second sister. "I told you how to pull it out."

"No, me!" shouted the youngest sister. "I told you the secret of the echo. Without that you could not have done it."

The sisters began to quarrel and fight with each other, pulling each other's hair and scratching each other's faces.

"Ladies, ladies," said Yendrik. "Where I come from, women shout in the field, but not in their homes. I find I cannot choose any of you." And he walked away, carrying his bag of apples.

The sisters looked at each other in fear. Their golden apples were all gone. How would they live? In the distance they heard Yendrik singing a song as he went along. As the song grew fainter and fainter, they began to weep. One by one they turned into thin, hazy clouds that went drifting around the tops of the mountains.

THE LAMB, THE TABLECLOTH, AND THE CLUB

This is, of course, very similar to the Grimm tale "The Magic Table, the Gold Donkey, and the Cudgel in a Sack." However, a number of scholars claim that this is an earlier version.

A cobbler went to church one day and heard the priest preach a sermon about "selling all you have and giving it to the poor and being rewarded a hundred-fold." The cobbler went home, determined to do just that. He told his wife his plans, and the poor woman loved her husband and trusted him, so she agreed.

He sold everything but his house and donated his money to the church to be given to the poor. Then he waited. And waited. And waited. But nothing happened. No reward came. He and his family became hungry. Their clothes started to look worn and shabby. He decided that perhaps he was supposed to go and look for his reward.

The cobbler walked slowly until he came upon a shepherd guarding a flock of lambs. He asked the shepherd if he had any food to share, and the shepherd invited him to sit down. While they ate, the cobbler told the shepherd what had happened in his life. "I wanted to give to the poor," he said sadly, "but I did not want to hurt my family."

At the end of the meal, the shepherd smiled and said, "I will give you one of my lambs. Whenever you need money, you must say 'Lamb, shake yourself.' You will get enough for yourself and your family. But I warn you, tell no one else about this."

The cobbler set off, carrying the lamb. In the afternoon, he decided to test the lamb to see if what the shepherd had said was true. He found a deserted field. "Lamb, shake yourself," he called out. Sure enough, the lamb gave a shake and there were golden coins at its feet, enough to pay for many meals. The cobbler was delighted. He continued on his way and then decided to stop at an inn to have some supper because his home was still quite far away.

In front of the inn he saw one of his gossipy neighbors. He asked her to watch over his lamb while he went inside to eat. "But whatever you do, don't shake her," said the cobbler. The neighbor looked at the lamb. She peeked inside the inn and saw the cobbler paying for his meal with a golden coin! She took the lamb to a quiet field behind the inn and shook it.

Nothing happened. In anger, she called out "Lamb, shake yourself!" and out poured some golden coins. Quickly, she ran to get a lamb from her flock that looked like the cobbler's lamb. She left the magic lamb in her flock and returned to the inn with the ordinary one. When the cobbler came out after eating, he took the lamb and went home.

The next day, the cobbler called his wife and children and told them to watch carefully. He placed the lamb in front of him and called out, "Lamb, shake yourself!" Nothing happened. He called out a second time, and then a third. Still nothing happened. He knew then that his special lamb had been stolen. For a time, he and his family lived on the gold that had come out of the lamb on the first shaking, but soon they were again without food.

Ashamed, the cobbler went back to the shepherd and told him what had happened. The shepherd simply smiled, shared his meal, and took a tablecloth out of his knapsack. He gave it to the cobbler and said, "When you or your family want something to eat, simply lay the cloth down and say 'Tablecloth, spread yourself!' It will soon be covered with food. But remember, tell no one about this."

Once again, on his way home the cobbler sat in the deserted field. "Tablecloth, spread yourself!" he commanded. The cloth rolled out, and soon it was covered with delicious food. He set off for home with the cloth under his arm. And once again he met his gossipy old neighbor. She took one look at the cloth he was carrying and said, "Let me hold that for you while you go in and have something to drink. You look very thirsty." The cobbler was indeed very thirsty, so he handed the cloth to her and said, "Whatever you do, don't spread it out."

The neighbor substituted a cloth of her own and put the magic one in her cupboard. She gave her cloth to the cobbler, and when he got home, he wanted to show its power to his wife and children. But when he placed it over his table and commanded it "Tablecloth, spread yourself!" nothing happened, just as before, with the sheep.

Full of shame, the cobbler went back to the shepherd. "I know now who has tricked me," he said. "It was my gossipy neighbor. Please help me to get back your earlier gifts." The shepherd was reluctant, but at last he handed the cobbler a small wooden club. It was decorated with silver and had a few jewels mounted at the top. The shepherd told the cobbler that if he gave the command "Club, move yourself!" the club would attack anyone nearby. When he wanted it to stop, he had to give it the command "Club, stop yourself."

The cobbler returned and confronted his gossipy neighbor. "Club, move yourself!" he commanded, and it began to attack his neighbor.

"I won't get it to stop until you have given me back my lamb and my tablecloth," said the cobbler. The neighbor ran to get them, and the cobbler ordered the club to stop.

He took his lamb, his tablecloth, and his club home, and he and his family lived happily for many years, always sharing their new wealth with the poor.

THE FORBIDDEN CHAMBER

This Bluebeard-like theme can be found in much of European folklore.

One day a wizard, disguised as a gentleman, came to the home of a woman who had three daughters. He asked to marry the eldest, and because he looked presentable, the mother allowed her daughter to marry him. After the wedding they went to the wizard's home.

The wizard had a special cat. He ordered his wife never to feed the cat while he was gone. Also, she was never to go into the room in the tower. If she did, she would die. The wizard then went on a trip to test his wife. He took a special mirror that allowed him to see what happened in his home at all times.

As soon as the wizard was gone, the cat began to meow. It meowed and meowed, never stopping for a moment. The wife just could not stand it. She fed the cat. As soon as the wizard saw this in his magic mirror, he raced home and put his wife to death. He put her body in one of the rooms in his house that he kept locked with a special key.

After a year had passed, he went to the same mother, in a different disguise, and asked to marry the second daughter. Again the mother agreed, and again the wizard took his wife home. The same thing happened. He went on a trip, watched in the mirror as this wife also fed the cat and started up to see what was in the forbidden room. He raced home to put her to death.

One more year passed. This time the wizard did not go in disguise. He simply told the mother that his wife had died, and he would now like to marry the third daughter. Once again the mother gave permission, and the wizard took his wife home. He went off on a trip and watched his wife. But she did not give in to the cat when it meowed and meowed. And she made no move to go to the tower room. When the wizard saw this, he said to himself, "At last, I have an obedient wife." He did not return home for a long time, and he forgot all about looking in the magic mirror.

Meanwhile, this wife found a strange set of keys. She went from room to room, trying out each key. In one room she found a large cupboard with magic ointments. At last she went up to the tower room. There she found the bodies of her sisters, and of many other women as well. They had been taken as wives earlier by the wizard. She smeared the magic ointments on all the women, and they came alive. They did not wait for the wizard to come back. They all went back to their homes. No one knows what happened to the wizard, for the next time they looked, his house had disappeared.

MAJKA

This unusual fairy tale was probably created in much the same way Hans Christian Andersen crafted many of his tales: by using folkloric themes and inventing unusual endings. This certainly has one of the most extraordinary acts of forgiveness to occur in a tale of this type.

*T*he King and Queen of the Golden Island died, leaving behind their only daughter, Majka. She was too young to take over and reign as queen, but before the court could decide what to do, her uncle surrounded the country with his army and said he would be the regent and act as guardian for Majka. He would give over the throne to her as soon as she came of age.

Secretly, however, the uncle planned to be the king. He placed her under the care of one of his most trusted servants, a man called Yust. Yust was known to be pitiless and hard-hearted. He was to keep her in a small house and dress her no better than a poor peasant. Her food was to be given to her in small portions, poorly cooked at that. It was obvious that the uncle hoped Princess Majka would die.

But in spite of her poor food and her lonely life, Majka grew up to be kind and uncomplaining. She grew to love Yust, even though he often seemed cold and unfeeling. Once in a while Yust would respond to her love, in spite of himself. He would slip her an extra piece of bread or meat.

One day Yust was sleeping in the garden when he was attacked by a colony of ants. Majka passed by and saw this. Carefully she picked off hundreds of the ants, one by one, so that they would not bother Yust, and crushed them into a pile. He woke up and saw what Majka had done, for her hands and fingers were covered with ant bites.

Yust kissed the hands of Princess Majka and told her he had a special gift for her. When he brought it out, she saw it was a tiny harmonica. Yust said that it had magic powers, but only in the hands of a good person. He had never been able to get it to work its magic.

After that, whenever Majka played the harmonica, the birds came out of the trees and fluttered all around her, whistling and chirping and twittering. Squirrels and snakes and other small creatures of the forest came and sat by her feet. They all became her best friends, and she would talk to them, especially to a raven that she made her special pet.

Her uncle knew nothing of this. Every day he expected to hear she was ill or dying. Yust told him that she was growing thinner every day, but it was not the truth.. When he heard Majka call him "Grandfather" every day, something was awakened in his cold heart. He came to love her as though she were truly his granddaughter.

Majka came of age, and everyone in the court told the regent uncle it was now time for her to be crowned queen. He rebelled and would not allow it. Finally he said, "I remind you that we have a law that says every new ruler must pass the three tests of patience, courage, and love. If the Princess can pass the tests I set before her, then I will allow her to be crowned queen."

He brought out a bushel of poppy seeds, mixed with fine gravel. He told Majka she must separate the seeds from the gravel in one day, to show she had patience. Everyone left the room, leaving Majka alone. She began to weep. Her pet raven, sitting at the window, heard her and asked what was the matter. Majka spoke of the challenge and pointed to the bushel.

The raven hurried off to the woods and called all the birds. They came twittering and chirping to the room where Majka sat. Soon their beaks had separated all of the pieces of gravel from the poppy seeds and left them in two piles.

When her uncle came into the room, expecting to find her in tears, he saw that she was smiling happily.

"I am pleased at your patience," said her uncle smoothly. "Now you must pass the test of courage." He had a huge chest brought in by one of the servants. The servant opened the chest and quickly ran out of the room, locking the door. Out from the chest slithered many snakes, all headed toward Majka. Quickly she took out her magic harmonica and began to play tune after tune. The snakes lifted their heads and began to sway to the music, as though they were dancing.

When her uncle entered the room some time later, he found her still playing, and the snakes dancing harmlessly in a circle around her. Her uncle was furious.

"Some evil magic has allowed you to pass the test of courage. But now comes the test of love. You must show us some proof of a love you have such as the world has never seen."

Princess Majka looked at her uncle and said, "Dear uncle, I love you as I loved my father, who was your brother. I know that you want the throne. And because I love you, I willingly give up the throne to you."

This was too much for the heart of her wicked uncle to bear. It stopped beating and he fell over, dead.

And so Majka passed the three tests and took her place as queen.

ARGELUS AND THE SWANS

This tale reverses many of the motifs found in similar European tales. It is rare to find a prince confined to a palace. Usually it is a princess. The theme of the princess and her handmaidens who have been turned into swans is reminiscent of the Grimm tale of the seven ravens who were brothers. A gypsy version can be found in the collection put together by Groome, in which it is titled "The Golden Bird and the Good Hare."

*T*here was once a king who had two sons. The older was called Argelus. He was so incredibly handsome and talented, his father made him live in his own private palace. In that way, he believed his son would not give in to the petty temptations of the court. It was fortunate Argelus had every comfort in his castle, because his father did not allow him to leave it, for fear he would come to harm.

One day in the garden of the palace, there sprang up a beautiful apple tree. On the morning it appeared, it had lovely golden blossoms; by nightfall, there were golden fruits on every branch. The king was delighted and called all of the most important nobles to come and have a look.

So that the fruit would not be stolen during the night, the king put a guard on duty. But the guard fell asleep, and all of the fruit had disappeared by morning. On the second night the king doubled the guard, but still the apples were gone by morning. The third night, the same thing happened. The king could not understand it, so he commanded a magician to find out what was causing the apples to disappear, and how it could be stopped.

The magician said, "If I tell you, you will kill me or put me away."

The king urged him to speak, saying he had nothing to fear. So the magician answered, "The tree is enchanted. Argelus is the only one who can guard it in such a way that the apples will not disappear."

Upon hearing this answer, the king grew very angry. "You rogue," he shouted. "You want my son to come to harm, but it is you who will suffer first." He cast the magician into a dungeon.

Now the second son of the king was a mischievous lad, and the king didn't like him very much. This son offered to watch over the tree, and the king agreed to it readily. But next morning the fruit was gone, as usual. The second son went to his brother Argelus and told him that he had failed. That night Argelus had a strange dream.

When the King came to see Argelus the next day, he noticed that his favorite son was troubled. He asked him what was the matter.

"I had a dream about the apple tree," answered Argelus. "I dreamed that someone told me I was the only one who could guard the tree and prevent the apples from being stolen. I want to stand guard tonight."

At first the king refused his request, but finally he agreed. Argelus had his bed, a table, and a lamp taken out and placed directly under the tree. He asked one of his servants to stay with him. Stretching out on the bed, he began to read a book.

Right at midnight, he saw seven swans fly to the tree and perch on its branches. Quickly he reached up and grabbed the largest of the swans. In that moment it turned into a pretty young girl. Immediately the six other swans turned into young girls and surrounded her. The first one to be transformed, the one Argelus had grabbed, said she was a princess who had been put under a spell. The others were her handmaidens.

Argelus was very moved. He and the princess spoke at length. She begged him to come and stay there two more nights. That was the only way she could be freed from her spell. Argelus promised her he would do so.

As soon as dawn broke, the girls turned back into swans and flew away. The apples were still on the tree. The king was very happy to see them and to see his son was safe. Argelus did not tell his father about the princess or the swans, nor did he mention his promise. He made his servant swear that he would keep silent as well.

But this servant was in love with the daughter of a witch. Secretly, he told his sweetheart what he had seen the night before. She told her mother. Her mother ordered the servant to tell no one else. Then she gave him a leather bag and a vial of oil.

"As soon as your master lies down on his bed, stand near his head and open the bag just a little. He will immediately fall asleep. As soon as the swans have flown away again at dawn, take some of the oil from the vial and spread it on his eyelids. He will wake up and never realize he has been asleep."

That night Argelus prepared himself to stay awake, as he had the night before. But the moment the servant opened the bag, he fell into a deep sleep. When the swans arrived and changed into human form, the princess tried to shake him awake, but he did not even flutter his eyelids. She asked the servant to help her, but he refused. As soon as the swans flew away at dawn, he smeared some of the oil on Argelus's eyelids, and he awoke. When he saw that the apples were gone, he was angry with himself for having failed to keep his promise to the princess.

On the third night the same thing happened. Even though he had tried to sleep all day so as to be awake at night, Argelus fell into the same deep sleep the moment the servant opened the leather bag near his eyes. Before the princess left at dawn, she said to the servant, "Tell your master that we must go far away, to the Dark City. And be sure to give him this message as well: He must move the sword that hangs over his bed to a different spot. Then he will know what to do."

As soon as Argelus awoke, he saw the apples were gone. Sadly, he went back inside his palace. Because his servant had given him the message about his sword, he took it down and was about to move it to a different spot. Immediately the sword twisted in his hands and pointed at the servant. Then Argelus knew he had been betrayed. He had the servant thrown into the dungeon.

He then told his father all about the swan maidens and said he wanted to go in search of them. His father did not want to let him go, but when he saw that Argelus was almost dying of grief, he relented. He gave him horses, a carriage, servants, food, and a lot of money.

For seven years Argelus searched for the Dark City. When all his money was gone, he sent his servants home. He traded his horses for food and shelter, and finally they were all gone as well. He continued his journey on foot, meeting many beggars. He learned from the beggars that one often had to use trickery to get the next meal or a place to stay the night.

One day he came upon three young brothers, fighting each other. When he asked why they were fighting, the oldest replied, "Our father left us only what you see here, this table, a horse, a saddle, and a whip. We don't know how to divide them up equally, because, you see, all those things are magic. Whoever puts the saddle on the horse, mounts it, and then cracks the whip, will be taken to wherever he wants to go. Then whoever gives the table a whack with his fist will bring back the horse, saddle, and whip."

"Why don't you let me help you decide?" said Argelus. "I come from a noble family and have some experience with magic." The brothers agreed to give it a try, so Argelus ordered each brother to climb to the top of three nearby hills. Then they were to race down, and the first one to come back to Argelus would get his choice of the inheritance.

The brothers set off, each in a different direction, and as soon as they were out of sight, Argelus saddled the horse, mounted it, cracked the whip, and said, "Take me to the Dark City." Off went the horse, and Argelus kept going until suddenly he was thrown into a swamp. For the three brothers had come back and seen that Argelus had taken the horse and saddle and whip. They had given the table a whack, and that brought the horse back to them.

Argelus went to a nearby inn and asked the innkeeper if he knew the way to the Dark City. The innkeeper said he did not, but many travelers and caravans passed by that way. Perhaps if he stayed there a few nights and asked each person who came by, one might know the way to the Dark City.

Argelus stayed at the inn three nights, asking each traveler who came, "Do you know the way to the Dark City?" No one knew. He was about to give up when a merchant said he knew it lay more than a hundred leagues farther east. Argelus gave the stranger the last thing of value he owned, a precious jewel, and begged him to lead the way to the Dark City.

The stranger agreed and said he would go only until the Dark City could be seen on the horizon. It was dangerous for him to go farther. He led Argelus to that point and left him there. Argelus walked the rest of the way to the Dark City, and when he arrived, he saw that a big celebration was being planned. The houses and streets were decorated with flowers and leafy branches. When Argelus asked what the occasion was, one of the townspeople said, "Today the princess is going to be married. She has been under a spell for seven years, but now it is over and she will marry in a few days."

Argelus went at once to the royal castle, but by now his clothes were shabby. The guards thought he was a beggar and would not let him in. He wandered back into the town, and suddenly he recognized one of the princess's handmaidens, buying something in the town square. He approached her and told her he was Argelus, who had been searching for them for seven years.

She ran back to the princess with the news, but the princess would not believe her. She sent a second handmaiden to meet with Argelus, who came back with the same account. Then she sent the third, the fourth, the fifth, and the sixth, and when they had all returned with the same story, saying they recognized Argelus, the princess was overjoyed. She ran to Argelus, and they fell in love all over again. She told her father she would marry the next week, but not the one he had planned for her. She wanted only to marry Argelus. When the old king died, the princess became queen and Argelus the king. He made a very good king, because in his seven years of travels, he had learned what few young princes learn: to have lost one's worldly goods does not mean one has lost the meaning and purpose of life.

PART 6

Chain Chants and Cumulative Tales

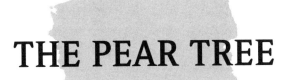

THE PEAR TREE

This chain tale is included to show its great similarity to such chain tales as the English "This Is the House That Jack Built." The nonsense words at the ends of the lines are provided phonetically, as they would sound in Polish.

God made pear tree, to give fine pears, eye vye bim bom bom.

Pear tree did not want to let go, eye vye, bim bom bom.

God made goat to shake the tree, eye vye bim bom bom.

Shake the pear tree!

Goat just would not shake the tree; tree would not let go of pears, eye vye bim bom bom.

God made dog to bite the goat, eye vye bim bom bom.

Bite the goat!

Dog just would not bite the goat; goat just would not shake the tree; tree would not let go of pears, eye vye bim bom bom

God made stick to beat the dog, eye vye bim bom bom.

Beat the dog!

Stick just would not beat the dog; dog just would not bite the goat; goat just would not shake the tree; tree would not let go of pears, aye vye bim bom bom.

God made fire to burn the stick, aye vye bim bom bom.

Burn the stick!

Fire just would not burn the stick; stick just would not beat the dog; dog just would not bite the goat; goat just would not shake the tree; tree would not let go of pears, aye vye bim bom bom.

God made water to quench the fire, aye vye bim bom bom.

Quench the fire!

Water would not quench the fire; fire just would not burn the stick; stick just would not beat the dog; dog just would not bite the goat; goat just would not shake the tree; tree would not let pears fall down, eye vye bim bom bom.

God made ox to drink the water, eye vye bim bom bom.

Drink the water!

Ox just would not drink the water; water just would not quench the fire; fire just would not burn the stick; stick just would not beat the dog; dog just would not bite the goat; goat just would not shake the tree; tree would not let go of pears, aye vye bim bom bom.

God made butcher to kill the ox, aye vye bim bom bom.

Kill the ox!

Butcher just would not kill the ox; ox just would not drink the water; water just would not quench the fire; fire just would not burn the stick; stick just would not beat the dog, dog just would not bit the goat; goat just would not shake the tree; tree would not let go of pears, aye vye bim bom bom.

God made Death to take the butcher.

Take the butcher!

Then butcher began to kill the ox, ox began to drink the water, water began to quench the fire, fire began to burn the stick, stick began to beat the dog, dog began to bite the goat, goat began to shake the tree, and tree let go of all the pears, aye vye bim bom bom.

HEN AND ROOSTER

This chain tale works very well when told in tandem by two tellers. The exact translation for the word given here as "fiber" is phloem, the inner bark of the tree. Because few would recognize this word, it seemed better to use a more familiar one. In this version Rooster dies, but in some versions he revives and crows, "Kee-kee-ree-kee." (See the explanation of the terms "Pan" and "Pani" in "The People" in part 1.)

*H*en and Rooster went to the forest to pick nuts. Every nut Hen found, she put in a basket. Every nut Rooster found, he put in his stomach. But one nut was too big. It stayed in his throat. Rooster couldn't breathe. He fell down in some nettles, gasping. Hen went to the sea and said, "Sea, Sea, give me water."

"For whom?"

"For poor Rooster in the nettles; quickly now, before death settles."

But the sea said, "You must go to the linden tree to get me fiber."

So Hen went to the linden tree and said, "Linden, linden give me fiber."

"For whom?"

"For the sea, so it will give me water."

"For whom?"

"For poor Rooster in the nettles; quickly now, before death settles."

But the linden tree said, "You must go to pig and ask him to dig around my roots."

So Hen went to pig and said, "Pig, pig, come and dig."

"For whom?"

"For the linden, so it will give me fiber."

"For whom?"

"For the sea, so it will give me water."

"For whom?"

"For poor Rooster in the nettles; quickly now, before death settles."

But the pig said, "You must go to the cow and get me milk to drink."

So Hen went to the cow and said, "Cow, cow, give me milk now!"

"For whom"

"For the pig, so he will dig."

"For whom?"

"For the linden, so it will give me fiber."

"For whom?"

"For the sea, so it will give me water."

"For whom?"

"For poor Rooster in the nettles; quickly now, before death settles."

But the cow said, "You must go to the cowherd to get me hay."

So Hen went to the cowherd and said, "Cowherd, cowherd, give me hay."

"For whom?"

"For the cow, so she will give me milk now."

"For whom?"

"For the pig, so he will dig."

"For whom?"

"For the linden, so it will give me fiber."

"For whom?"

"For the sea, so it will give me water."

"For whom?"

"For poor Rooster in the nettles; quickly now, before death settles."

But the cowherd said to Hen, "You must go to the Pani and ask her for some cheese."

So Hen went to the Pani and said, "Pani, pani, give me cheese."

"For whom?"

"For the cowherd, so he'll give hay."

"For whom?"

"For the cow, so she'll give milk now."

"For whom?"

"For the pig, so he will dig."

"For whom?"

"For the linden, so it will give fiber."

"For whom?"

"For the sea, so it will give water."

"For whom?"

"For poor Rooster in the nettles; quickly now, before death settles."

But the Pani said, "You must find my needle, then I will give you cheese."

Hen looked and looked and looked and found the needle. Hen gave the needle to Pani. Pani gave Hen cheese. Hen gave the cheese to the cowherd. Cowherd gave Hen some hay. Hen gave the hay to the cow. Cow gave milk to Hen. Hen gave the milk to the pig. Pig went to the linden tree to dig. The linden tree gave Hen some fiber. Hen gave the fiber to the sea. The sea gave Hen some water. Hen went to Rooster and gave him the water.

But poor rooster did not waken, no matter how much he was shaken.

ELE MELE JOEY

This charming Polish Jewish chain tale would also suit tandem tellers. For those who wish to tell this in both languages, the original words, in Polish Yiddish, can be found in the "Sources."

*E*le, mele Joey (Josiek), you have a black-haired fiancee.

She is wearing red shoes; she is standing by a tree.

Why is she standing by a tree?

To collect the leaves.

Why is she collecting leaves?

To give to the cow.

Why does the cow need leaves?

To eat them so it can give milk.

For what do you need milk?

To give to the children to drink.

Why do the children need to drink milk?

So they can collect stones.

Why do they need to collect stones?

To build a little temple.

Why do they want to build a little temple?

To sing psalms.

Why do they sing psalms?

To have a happy future.

THE HAIRY, HORNED GOAT

Known throughout Europe, this tale is often recited as a chant or even sung. Some variants have the rabbit, rather than the fox, as the creature whose den is occupied, and it is only an ant that saves them all from the hairy horned goat.

*T*here was once a hairy, horned Goat who was always angry. She would butt with her horns, stamp with her front feet, and threaten anyone who came near. As soon as anyone approached, she would bleat in her loudest voice:

"I'm a hairy, horned Goat; if you touch me you will regret it. I will stamp you with my feet, butt you with my horns, eat you to the last bit."

The Goat grew bold and raided gardens, stamping on and damaging whatever she did not eat. One day she went into the garden of a tailor. When he saw her among his cabbages, he took his longest, sharpest scissors and ran out to the Goat, shouting, "Do you think I am afraid of you?"

The Goat saw the tailor; she saw the giant scissors, opening and closing like a big trap. She ran faster on her four legs than the tailor could run on his two, and escaped his shears. She kept on running until she came to a forest, where she saw a den. She decided to stay there so the tailor could not find her. She did not know it was the den belonging to Mr. and Mrs. Fox.

Mrs. Fox came home and was about to enter the den when she heard a noise from within. "Who is in there?" she called angrily.

The Goat called back in her fiercest voice:

"It is I, the hairy, horned Goat. If you touch me you will regret it. I will stamp you with my feet, butt you with my horns, eat you up to the last bit."

Soon Mr. Fox came home and saw his wife, weeping and howling. When he asked her why, she said, "Some monster is in our den and threatens to eat us up."

"I will make that monster come out," bragged Mr. Fox. "Who is in there?" he barked in his loudest voice. The Goat answered him in an even louder voice:

"It is I, the hairy, horned Goat. If you touch me, you will regret it. I will stamp you with my feet; butt you with my horns, eat you up to the last bit."

Mr. Fox lowered his tail between his legs, and he and Mrs. Fox ran off into a different part of the forest, crying and wailing. They met Mr. Rabbit. He was astonished to see them crying. Mr. Fox pretended it was just something caught in his eye, but Mrs. Fox told all about the monster in their den. Mr. Rabbit sped off to the den so fast the Foxes could not keep up.

"Who is in there? Come right out!" ordered Mr. Rabbit.

"It is I, the hairy, horned Goat. If you touch me you will regret it. I will stamp you with my feet, butt you with my horns, eat you up to the last bit."

Mr. Rabbit and the Foxes went to Mr. Wolf. As soon as he heard their story, he gnashed his teeth and said, "You will soon be sleeping in your den. Lead me to it." When they got there, Mr. Wolf called out, "Who is in there? Come out at once."

"It is I, the hairy, horned Goat. If you touch me you will regret it. I will stamp you with my feet; butt you with my horns, eat you up to the last bit."

When Mr. Wolf heard that, he flattened his ears and said it was too much for him. Mr. and Mrs. Fox, Mr. Rabbit, and Mr. Wolf continued on their way, howling and yowling. They met Mr. Bear, lumbering along in the forest. One side of his face was all swollen because it had been stung by many bees, but Mr. Bear did not care, he had managed to eat a lot of honey. He stopped to ask why they were making such a racket. When he heard their story, Mr. Bear just laughed.

"All right, I'll take care of that hairy, horned Goat. But first I must find my two helpers." He searched until he found Mr. Crab and Mr. Hedgehog. They set off for the den, and when they got there Mr. Bear called out in his deep, gruff voice, "How are you doing in there, Nanny Goat?" The Goat was frightened. She had never heard such a gruff voice before. Still, she called out as loud as she could:

"I'm the hairy, horned Goat. If you touch me you will regret it. I will stamp you with my feet, butt you with my horns, eat you up to the last bit."

"Eat up, then," laughed Mr. Bear. "I will send you two to start on." He told Mr. Crab and Mr. Hedgehog to go into the den. He ordered Mr. Fox to wait with him, right at the mouth of the den. Mr. and Mrs. Fox were to wait at the top of the hill, in case the Goat got past Mr. Wolf. Mr. Rabbit, being the fastest of all, was to wait on the other side of the hill and follow her if she should get that far.

"I am Mr. Crab, and this is the way I pinch," said Mr. Crab as soon as he had entered the den. He pinched the Goat with all his strength.

"I am Mr. Hedgehog, and this is how I prick," said Mr. Hedgehog, and he sent his sharp needles into the tender belly of the Goat.

"Ow, ow, ow," bleated the Goat, and she came bounding out of the den. She came out so fast she whisked right by Mr. Bear and Mr. Wolf. She even ran past Mr. and Mrs. Fox so swiftly that they could not touch her. But when she came to Mr. Rabbit, he jumped on her back and hung on for dear life. The other animals finally caught up. The Goat could see she did not have a chance against so many.

"You are not fair," she bleated. "There are seven of you against me. If you wish to make war, you must let me get my army together so it is a more equal fight. Give me three days, and we will meet again, right here." The other animals were so astonished, before they could agree or disagree, the Goat bounded off.

The Goat asked many animals to join her, but none would. At last she met Mr. Dog, who said he would come because he was at war with his master and mistress. The Goat said they would need more animals to join with them.

"I know who to ask," insisted Mr. Dog. Sure enough, he found Mr. Cat and Mr. Rooster, and both of them looked as though they were not afraid of anything.

For three days the other animals had waited. They had given up hope that the Goat would return. Mr. Bear climbed a tree to look off in the distance. "They're coming! They're coming," he shouted. "I can barely see them, but I hear them. It sounds like a fierce army. One is shouting that he can smell our tracks; another is screaming something that sounds like 'Hee, hee, hee, let me at all three.' And he seems to be carrying a rough-edged sword on his head that is already covered with blood. I'm not coming down from this tree. I'll stay right here and direct the fighting."

When they heard what Mr. Bear said, Mr. Wolf ran off as though he had been shot, and Mr. Fox climbed under a piece of mossy ground. But his tail stuck out, and Mr. Cat jumped on it, scratching with his claws. Mr. Fox jumped out, and that scared Mr. Cat so much he gave a shriek and started climbing up the tree where Mr. Bear was hiding.

"They're after me," growled Mr. Bear. He let go of the branch on which he was sitting and fell down with such a thud it made the earth shake. Both armies turned and ran. When Mr. Bear got up, his sides were aching. Suddenly he heard the Goat bleating nearby. Mr. Rabbit was again clinging to her back, just as he had before.

"I will not let you go," he shouted. "You must be punished."

Just then Mr. Bear came up. "Please, Mr. Rabbit, come and massage my sides with a bit of mosquito fat. They hurt so much I cannot stand it."

Kind Mr. Rabbit jumped off and went to massage Mr. Bear. That was all the Goat needed. She took off and ran as she had never run before. She ran one day, she ran two days, she ran three days. Maybe she is running still. And that was the end of her bad behavior, and the two armies never did get together to fight it out.

PART 7

Humorous Tales

THE GOOSE WITH ONE LEG

In many tales, the peasant or servant tries to get the better of a person from the nobility. This is a typical example.

*T*here was once a nobleman who had a very good cook. The trouble was, this cook loved to eat. He could not resist taking bites, or even big portions, of the food he cooked for the nobleman and his family.

One day the cook roasted a big, plump goose. The crispy skin of the goose glistened. The cook simply could not resist. He tore off one of the legs and ate the whole thing. When he took the goose in to the nobleman for his dinner, the nobleman was upset.

"What happened to the other leg?" he asked. He suspected that the cook had eaten it.

"Oh, this goose had only one leg," answered the cook. "There are many geese with only one leg."

The nobleman did not think this was likely and wanted to punish the cook, but he knew that if he did, the cook was likely to go elsewhere to work. And he was an excellent cook. But he vowed to watch the cook more carefully after this.

A few days later, the cook was going with the nobleman to purchase food for a feast. It was very cold, and ice had formed on the pond near the nobleman's house. There stood the geese, each on one leg and with the other leg tucked under a wing to keep it warm.

"You see," said the cook. "It is just as I told you. There are many geese with only one leg."

The nobleman put two fingers in his mouth and gave a sharp, piercing whistle. The flock of geese put down their legs, lifted their wings, and flew off.

"Well, my dear jester cook. Did you see that? Did those geese have one leg or two?"

"Well, you see, sir, if you had whistled at the goose I cooked before I cooked it, it would have had two legs as well, but you did not whistle. So the goose had only one leg."

THE PRINCESS WHO WOULD
NOT LAUGH

*T*here was once a princess who could not bring herself to laugh. Her parents were very sad that their daughter acted like a cold and heartless statue whenever a young man came to court her or even just tried to be friends with her. The parents announced that whoever could make their daughter laugh would be allowed to ask for her hand in marriage. The princess was rich and beautiful, so many a young man attempted to make her laugh. But not one succeeded. Some even lost their lives trying.

There was a king in a neighboring land who had three sons. The two oldest were very learned, but the youngest was a simpleton. The oldest came to his father one day and said, "Give me my inheritance so I can put on a good show to win over that princess."

The king resisted at first because this son was the wisest and would be first in line for the throne. But the oldest son insisted and at last convinced his father to give in. The prince set off with a good amount of food and money. He also carried a jingly rattle, and being very overconfident, was sure he could make the princess laugh. On the way to the princess's palace, he stopped by a well to get a drink. An old man sat on the edge of the well and stopped the prince from taking a drink.

"Please, can you spare a bit of bread?" asked the old man.

"Get out of my way, old man," shouted the prince, "or I'll beat you up with my walking stick." The old man walked away, and the prince took a drink of water and continued on his way.

As soon as he arrived at the palace, he asked to see the princess. When she entered the room, he began to shake the rattle and grin at her. The princess did not look at him, nor did she even smile. And that was the end of his rattling.

Some time later his brother, the second wise prince, said to his father, "Give me my inheritance so I can try for the hand of the princess. I will take a rolling pin and use it as though it were a king's scepter. If I dress in jester's clothing, she will surely think that is amusing and give a good laugh." Just like his brother, he set off with food and money, carrying the rolling pin majestically, as though it were a king's scepter. And just like his brother, he arrived at that same well, and there was the same old man.

"Please, can you spare a bit of bread?" asked the old man.

"Away with you, old man, or I'll beat you with my scepter so hard you won't know where you are."

The old man left, and the prince drank some water and continued on his way. Before he entered the princess's palace, he dressed himself in jester's clothes, carrying the rolling pin as though it were made of gold and decorated with jewels. He capered before the princess, but she did not even smile, much less laugh. And that was the end of his capering.

Finally, the third son, the simpleton, said to his father, "Father, permit me to go to that palace where the princess who never laughs lives."

"You foolish one, you can go to the four winds for all I care," answered his father, and he sent his son on his way without a penny. A kind maidservant offered the young man some dried biscuits for the journey. He went along until he came to that same well, where the same old man sat as before.

"May God be with you, old grandfather," said the youngest son as he sat down.

"Please, can you spare a bit of bread?" asked the old man.

"I have no bread, grandfather, but I have some dried biscuits. If your teeth are strong enough to chew them, you are welcome to share them with me."

They shared the biscuits and drank some water. After that the young man fell into a deep sleep. He dreamed that a golden carriage stood before him, pulled by a golden goose and a golden gander.

"Get up!" called the old man. "I come as an angel of God to reward you for your kindness."

The youngest prince started awake and saw the carriage of his dreams, with a golden goose and gander harnessed to it and ready to pull it along. He got into the carriage, and off they went to the palace of the princess. Everyone they passed stared in astonishment. He stopped at an inn to have something to eat. Two of the innkeeper's daughters had just stepped out to the carriage house. They had taken off their dresses to shake out the fleas and get ready for a bath. One of the daughters saw the golden carriage and had an idea. She grabbed a knife and began to scrape at the gold on the back of the carriage, trying to take off some of the gold. But soon she realized that she was stuck fast to the back of the carriage. The more she tried to scrape free, the harder she was stuck.

The youngest prince did not see her. When he had finished eating, he got into his carriage and set off, with the girl stumbling along behind, moaning and groaning. They passed a bakery, where the baker looked up to see what was causing such a commotion. The baker was so astounded at seeing the carriage with the half-naked girl attached to the back that he forgot to take out his bread and it got burnt.

"You rascal," he shouted at the girl, "because of you my bread got burned." He chased after her with his baking paddle and began to spank her. The moment he touched her, he, too, was stuck fast.

The carriage rolled on, with the half-naked girl and the baker stumbling along behind. It crossed a bridge over a river. At the edge of the river was a washerwoman, rinsing out the clothes she had washed. When she looked up and saw them and the carriage, she was so dumbfounded that she forgot to watch what she was doing. Soon the current carried away all her laundry. She took her laundry paddle and ran after the carriage.

"You rascals, you made me lose my laundry," she shouted at them. She began to paddle the baker and the half-naked innkeeper's daughter. As soon as she had touched them, she stuck fast.

The carriage rolled on, followed by the half-naked innkeeper's daughter, the baker, and the washerwoman. They appeared at the palace, and soon there was a hullabaloo, with everyone laughing and pointing at the funny sight. The princess appeared on her balcony and saw the golden carriage pulled by a golden goose and gander, the simpleton prince waving at her from a carriage window, the half-naked innkeeper's daughter, the baker shouting about his burnt bread, and the washerwoman screaming about her lost laundry.

First the princess smiled, then she laughed, and then she laughed some more. Indeed, she guffawed and shrieked from pure enjoyment, laughing until the tears flowed down her cheeks.

So it was that the simpleton prince won the princess, and to the end of their days, he could always make her laugh.

THE KING AND THE CAPTAIN

Tale telling in which exaggeration is used in a matter-of-fact manner, as though it could really be true, is a very old tradition. For many years, in the town of Moncrabeau, Gascony (France), there has been a festival featuring such storytelling. It is held each August and is sponsored by the local "Liars' Academy." The captain and his sergeant, from this story, would surely have been winners.

*T*here was once a King who had two daughters. He loved to joke and exaggerate and tell stories that could not possibly be true. But he no longer found anyone in his kingdom who would exchange braggardly tales with him. He decided to let it be known that he would give his daughters in marriage to anyone who could fabricate better lies than he could. Young men came from all over, but none of them told bigger, more interesting whoppers than he.

News of the King's challenge came to the ears of a military captain who had just been released from his duties. He called his sergeant, Jerome, and said, "Let's go there and try our luck." On the way they happened to see a metal hoop floating in the water.

"Look, Jerome! How strange! That metal hoop floats. It should sink, don't you think?" asked the Captain.

"Oh, no, dear Captain. I don't think it is a metal hoop. I believe it is a millstone."

"Sergeant Jerome, I think you will be a big help to me when we get to the King's palace. Come along."

They arrived at the palace, and the King invited the Captain to dinner. Sergeant Jerome went off to take care of their horses. The King and the Captain chatted a while, then suddenly six servants arrived, carrying a giant cabbage.

"In your country, do you have cabbages as big as this?" asked the King.

"Well," said the Captain, "when I served in my military unit, I was in charge of two platoons, and I never needed more than one cabbage to feed all of them at one meal."

The King expressed his doubt at this claim, but the Captain told him to call in his sergeant to verify what he had said. Sergeant Jerome came and the King asked, "Jerome, is it true that your Captain needed only one cabbage to feed his two platoons?"

"Oh no, dear King," replied Jerome. "I would not know about that. I did not serve the Captain until after that. But I have to say that in our area, we just order one cabbage for the whole winter. Everyone eats what they want, and in spring there are still two barrels of sauerkraut left over. We also have enough to feed ten cows."

"Oh," said the King. "Is that so? Well, you can go now."

The King and the Captain began to chat again. Suddenly there entered eight persons carrying a giant cucumber.

"Do you have such giant cucumbers in your place?" asked the King.

"Well, dear King," said the Captain slowly, "I am not sure about growing them, but once I was standing with my platoons by the side of a wide river. We had to get across, but there were no ferries or boats. We did have one cucumber, and so I gave orders to have it sliced in half, the long way. We hollowed out each half and saved the seeds, which we used as oars. Even though that river had a very swift current, we all crossed safely in those cucumber boats."

Once again the King doubted the Captain's story, but the Captain assured him that his Sergeant could verify it. So the King called Jerome again and asked him if it were true.

"Dear King, I wasn't there at exactly that time, but I do know that in our area, the cucumbers do grow very big. One day my master invited six men to go hunting, and each man had two servants, and each servant was in charge of three hunting dogs. They all went hunting one day, and everybody saw a rabbit running away. The dogs ran after the rabbit, and the servants ran after the dogs, and the hunters ran after their servants. The rabbit entered a hole in one end of a cucumber, and they all followed it in. It was so big they all got lost and did not come out until evening. They never did find the rabbit."

"Very well," said the King. "You may go. We will call again if we need you."

Now the King wanted to show the Captain his palace. He took him through all the rooms and asked, "In your place, do you have a palace as fine and big as this one?"

"Well, dear King, all I know is that once when we were building a house, one of the men dropped an axe. It fell down. He went down to look for it and did not get back to work at the top until evening. If you don't believe me, call my sergeant."

So the King called in the sergeant.

"Listen, Jerome, is that really true, what your Captain said about the builders?"

"Dear King, I wasn't there at that time. When I arrived the manor house was already built. But I do know that one night some hens happened to get to the very top of it, and they started to peck at the stars. Then the rooster arrived, and he began to gobble up the moon. Look up and you will see that it is more than halfway eaten away."

The King looked up and saw the crescent moon. Then he gave a big laugh and said, "Both of you are bigger liars than I will ever be. You may marry my daughters, if they will have you." So the Captain and Jerome married the two princesses, and I do believe they are still telling tall tales and making everyone laugh.

COBBLER KOPYTKO AND HIS DUCK KWAK

This is only the first part of a much longer tale. Kopytko means "little last," referring to the shoemaker's last. The panorama referred to in the first paragraph was an early form of picture show, telling stories by means of a large, rolled series of pictures.

*L*isten to what happened a hundred and fifty years ago. I saw it with my own eyes. In a town so big it had its own panorama, there lived a cobbler's apprentice whose name was Kopytko. He was so funny it was impossible to look at him without laughing. He would play tricks instead of mending shoes. Each time he played a trick, his master would pull one of his ears. This happened so often that his ears got to be as big as those of an elephant. But Kopytoko was glad of that because he could keep a lot of things in his big ears.

In his right ear he had a knife, buttons, chestnuts, and a spool of thread. In his left ear he kept a piece of pitch, a slingshot, and twenty small stones. You know he must have been a naughty youngster if he kept a slingshot and stones.

One evening Kopytko shot a stone so high it hit the moon in its face and knocked out the two front teeth. The poor moon had to hide its face behind the clouds for a night or two. When it reappeared again, it seemed to have a bandage on its face and was no longer smiling.

One time, Kopytko made shoes for a man who was always in a hurry. And do you know what he did? He put the heels where the toes should be and the toes where the heels should be. The man put on his shoes and started to go home to his dinner, but every time he tried to take a step forward, he went backward instead. He could not move from the spot for a long time and almost died of hunger. Kopytko laughed at him until his ears shook.

Sometimes, as punishment, Kopytko did not get any dinner from his master. But that seemed a small punishment for the mean thing he did once to a kind old gentleman. This man came to be measured for new shoes. He had very big feet, so the master called all of his apprentices to help him with the measuring tape. When no one was looking, Kopytko put a crab into the man's pocket. The crab ate a handkerchief, a pair of gloves, and a newspaper.

Cobbler Kopytko and His Duck Kwak   **153**

When the man put his hand into that pocket, the crab bit one of his fingers. The man shouted so loud, and the crab squeaked so shrilly, that the master ran away and did not come back.

Kopytko was now left on his own, so he decided to go away. He took with him some of the shoemaker's supplies. He wandered on until he met an enormous duck—a drake. The duck was staggering toward him.

"Why are you waddling like that?" asked Kopytko.

"I am a bit tipsy," said the duck.

"What's your name?' asked Kopytko,

"Kwak!" answered the duck.

"Well, come along with me and we can be merry together," said Kopytko.

"Where are you going?" asked Kwak.

"I'm trying to find a shoemaker, so I can finish my apprenticeship," answered Kopytko.

"All right, I'll go with you," said Kwak. "I have never seen ears like yours before."

Then went along together, playing tricks wherever they stopped. Kwak was as mischievous as Kopytko, perhaps even more so. They walked on and on, until they came to an old man lying down under a tree and fast asleep. He looked like a kindly person because he smiled sweetly in his sleep. Kopytko and Kwak began to plan how they could trick him.

Kopytko quietly approached the man, took off his shoes, tied them to a long piece of his shoemaker's thread, and strung the shoes up over a high branch of the tree. They waited until the man woke up. He looked around, and when he could not find his shoes, he was sure they were stolen. He grew sad and a few tears fell down his cheeks. Suddenly he looked up and saw his shoes hanging in the air above him. He stretched out his hand to pull them down, but the shoes slid up high into the air. Then they came down again, and once more the man tried to grasp them, but again the shoes went back up high. The old man sat down and began to cry bitterly. The tears poured down his face.

Kopytko, who was hiding behind the tree, whispered to Kwak, "What is happening to his eyes?"

"I don't know," answered Kwak, "but they seem to be quite wet."

"That's the first time I have seen that," said Kopytko. He was so overcome with curiosity that he came out from behind the tree and approached the old man.

"Oh misery and misfortune," cried the old man.

"What has happened?" asked Kopytko.

"My shoes have run away, and they won't come back. I have no money to buy another pair."

"I will bring your shoes back to you," said Kopytko, "if you tell me what that is coming from your eyes."

"Those are tears," answered the old man. "Did you never weep?"

"I don't know how," said Kopytko.

"Do you know how to laugh?"

"Oh, that I can do very well. I do it all the time." He ran behind the tree and brought the old man his shoes. Following him came Kwak.

"Why did you take them from me? Do you need a pair of shoes?'

"No."

"Then why did you do it?"

"To do mischief and give myself a good laugh."

"But that is what caused me to shed tears."

"Do those tears hurt you when you weep?"

"Yes, they hurt very badly. That is why one should never cause others to cry. Now, come near me."

"Are you going to hit me because I played a trick on you?"

"No, I wish to hug you and ask you never to play such tricks that make others cry. Come near me."

Kopytko approached him carefully. The old man patted him on the head and kissed him on both cheeks.

"What is this?" asked Kopytko in wonder as he felt something on his cheeks.

"Those are tears, and that means you have learned to cry."

"But you told me that tears cause pain, and these don't hurt me. In fact, they feel quite nice."

"That's because they are tears of joy. When you are very, very happy, you often cry tears of joy. Please don't play any more tricks that cause tears of pain."

"But I have always been merry. It is the way I am."

"That is fine," said the old man. "It is good to be merry and bring laughter to the world. Just don't bring it at someone else's expense. From now on, do your tricks and merrymaking out in the open, *for* others but not *to* others. You will see how much fun you can have." The old man went off with a smile.

"I liked that old man," said Kwak.

Kopytko and Kwak walked on until they came to the edge of a forest. There stood two children, crying because they had lost their way.

"Go near them and dance on one foot," Kopytko ordered Kwak. "I will stand on my head and kick my feet." They danced and kicked until the children stopped crying and started laughing. Then they helped the children find their way home. The parents hugged and kissed Kopytko and Kwak and gave them something to eat. Both of them felt really good.

They continued on their way and met a beggar, sitting at a crossroads and moaning.

"What's the matter?" asked Kopytko.

"I'm hungry and unhappy."

Kopytko reached into his ears, but he could find no food. Then he ordered Kwak to dance the Krakowiak, a lively dance. Kwak put out one of his feet and turned in a circle on the other. He turned and capered so much the beggar started to laugh. He laughed so hard he forgot he was hungry.

"How strange, he seems to have satisfied his hunger with laughter. Can laughter be eaten, I wonder?" said Kwak.

"It seems to be very healthy," answered Kopytko.

Thus they traveled for weeks and months. Whenever they heard of a person suffering sadness or sorrow, they went as quickly as possible to cheer up that person. In a short time, they became famous in the whole country and were blessed everywhere.

HOW THE PAPAJE MADE A JOURNEY

The term "Papaje" represents the petty nobility who were granted land and some status, either through inheritance or for service to a king. But some were so uneducated, they didn't know very much about the ways of the world. In all of the stories about them, they are easily duped or tricked. This tale comes from Ciechanow.

A long time ago, salt was very precious because it was difficult to get. Sometimes it had to be carted from a long distance away. People would do anything they could to get salt, because it made their food taste so much better.

The Papaje had heard of this wonderful product, and one or two of them had even tasted it. One day they heard that there was a source of salt in a part of the country that lay to the west of their lands. All the men in their group decided to go and find some salt. They gathered together all their horses, carriages, and carts and set off, leaving all the women and children behind.

Because they were heading west, they decided to leave in the afternoon so they could follow the setting sun. In that way, they knew they would always be going in the right direction. They were sure they could arrive by nightfall.

The roads were rough, and the horses had to walk slowly because they were not well fed. The Papaje had had no grain to feed them, only hay. They arrived at the edge of a forest just as the sun was setting. They were hot and thirsty and tired. They saw a shoemaker coming along the road from the direction in which they were headed. They asked him if it was still far to get the place where the salt could be found.

"Even if you set off now and rode all night, you would not get there until noon tomorrow," answered the shoemaker. "I have just come from there and I know exactly how far it is. It would be better if you rested here for the night and set off early tomorrow morning."

The Papaje were pleased with this answer. It was just what they wanted to do. They invited the shoemaker to sit down and share the food they had brought with them. He was very hungry and ate a lot. Then he told them stories of all the wonders of the town where the salt was to be found. Because he was a trickster and could see that the Papaje were very gullible, he had an idea.

"Gather your carts and carriages here, tight together, so no one can come upon you in the night and steal your things," he said. He showed them how to line up closely, all facing in the direction in which they would have to go in the morning. Then he found an anthill nearby, stuck a stick in the center of it, and told the Papaje men to lie around it in a circle, with their heads toward the anthill. The Papaje liked this idea. Each of the men could see someone familiar lying next to him, and in that way they would not be afraid. Happy and quiet, they all fell sound asleep.

The ants came out and began to crawl over the men, but they did not awaken, thinking it was only fleas. Some even murmured that it must be a popular place to sleep, there were so many fleas. While the Papaje slept, the shoemaker quietly turned around all of their carts and carriages, so they were all facing in the direction from which they had come.

The shoemaker called to the Papaje to get up. The sleepy nobles got up and set off. After several hours, they thought they should be near their goal.

"Look!" said one. "It is very similar to our area. There are even cows like ours."

They saw smoke rising from some small houses. The youngest Papaje said contemptuously, "What kind of town is this? It is no better than ours. The houses look just like ours. The women are dressed just like ours. I thought they would be more fashionable."

The women and children came out to welcome back their husbands and sons, eager to hear news of the bigger town, and how much salt they had been able to bring back. Just then one of the older men, not recognizing the women, called out, "Hey, good woman! Where can we buy some salt?"

What happened next is a bit difficult to describe. Many of the women did not recognize their husbands or sons because their faces were still so swollen from the ant bites. But when the dust had settled and both sides recognized each other, they all agreed they had never known of such stupidity in all their lives.

THE VERY SMART SON

The pseudo-Latin words that the son learns in school are just nonsense, but should be pronounced solemnly as if they were Church Latin.

One day a father who had never been to school decided that his son, at least, should learn how to read and write and do simple arithmetic. He took his son off to a school nearby and said to the teacher, "If you want my son to continue in this school, you must teach him something on the very first day, and something on every day after that. If you cannot, I will not pay his fees and he will no longer go to school."

"That will be very difficult; I cannot predict how your son will learn," explained the teacher. But the father insisted so the teacher said he would try.

That day, the teacher tried to teach the boy some basic Latin phrases, but he had never heard them before. When the boy returned from school that day, his father asked him what he had learned.

The young boy could not remember the Latin phrases his teacher had spoken, so he simply made up a sentence that sounded like those Latin words.

"I learned: *dimes komines, kurus gugurus, krowantum rogantum, suchom chrostom*," answered the boy.

The father did not understand at all, but the mother, when she heard her son speaking like that, said, "Just imagine! He learned so much Latin the first day, he sounds just like a priest. I think we should leave him in that school."

THE INHERITANCE OF A CAT

This is typical of the type of story that depends on a misunderstanding of words spoken in one language but heard as though spoken in another. Was is pronounced "vass," with the "a" sounding like ah.

$\mathcal{I}$n the Pomeranian part of Poland, where many people spoke German, there lived a father and his two sons. The father was rather poor. His wife had died, and soon he knew his time on earth was also coming to an end. He called his sons to him and said, "I have almost nothing to leave you except our cat. But she is worth a lot if you know where to take her. You will be able to earn good money."

Before the father could explain further, he died. The sons tried to sell the cat in their area, but everyone there already had a cat. No one was interested in buying another. So they put the cat in a bag and started out to find a place where they could sell the cat. They walked and walked until they came to a country they had never even heard of. As soon as they had entered the village, they saw mice running all around them. The mice seemed to be afraid of no one.

"Why don't you get rid of these mice?" asked the brothers, speaking Polish as best they could.

"We have tried," said the mayor, "but no matter what we do, they come back. They are so bold they steal the food off our plates."

"We have magic animal; help you get rid of the mice," said the oldest brother. "We sell it to you, for much money."

"We will pay you anything you ask," said the mayor. "But first we must have a demonstration that the animal really gets rid of mice."

The brothers let the cat out of the bag, and all the villagers were astonished to see it chase after the mice and kill them. The cat brought each dead mouse back to the brothers. The mayor and the villagers were satisfied that the cat really worked. They paid the brothers a lot of money, and the brothers set off to return home.

For a few hours the villagers could only watch in wonder as the cat continued to chase the mice and kill them. Soon there were few mice left. Then the villagers began to wonder:

What will the cat eat after all the mice were gone? They had forgotten to ask the brothers. One of the villagers hastily saddled his horse and chased after the brothers. He saw that they had crossed the river and were camped on the other side.

"What are we supposed to feed the cat?" shouted the village man. The brothers, listening from across the river, could not understand him.

"*Was?*" shouted the older brother in response. Now "*was*" in German means "what" but in Polish, "*was*" means "you," in the plural. When the man heard what the brother said, he thought it meant the cat would start eating all of the villagers. He raced back on his horse and told them they must lock the cat up in a room somewhere until they could figure out what to do. The people were afraid. They left the cat in the room for two days, trying to think of something they could do.

The cat was thirsty after all his hunting. He began to meow and meow, first softly and then louder and louder. No one came to open the door. The cat jumped up to the window. In the yard was a woodcutter chopping wood with an axe. When he saw the cat at the window, he was frightened and thought it was trying to get at him. The woodcutter threw his axe at the cat, but the cat jumped away. Now the window was broken, so the cat could jump out. This frightened the woodcutter so much, he climbed up the nearest tree.

The cat was ready to run away, but just then a dog came chasing after him. The cat ran up the same tree as the woodcutter. When the other villagers saw this, they were more frightened than ever. They decided to surround the tree with straw and branches and burn it down.

"What about me?" asked the woodcutter. "Do you want to burn me as well?" While they stood around thinking what to do, the cat jumped down and ran off in the direction from which he had come. He managed to find his way back to the two brothers, who were now rich and happy to have their cat back.

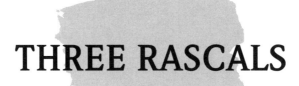

THREE RASCALS

*O*ne day a nobleman who owned a parrot accidentally let the parrot escape. He missed his parrot terribly and let it be known he would pay a big reward to the person who could find the parrot and bring it back. A poor old man came along and said he would try.

The old man walked into a nearby forest and in the distance heard a funny voice chattering the same words over and over. He was sure it was the parrot. He crept up to the hut, and there he saw three rascals teasing the parrot. As soon as it was dark and the fire was out, the old man climbed up to the roof and let himself down the chimney with a rope. He stole into the room and took the parrot. But as he tried to escape up the chimney again, the parrot started to squawk. The three rascals woke up, caught the old man by the legs, and pulled him down again.

The first rascal said, "We should kill him."

The second said, "We should cut him with a knife."

The third said, "We can fatten him up and eat him."

The rascals tied him up next to the parrot. The next morning two of them went off to the forest to chop wood. The third stayed behind to watch the old man and the parrot. But he fell asleep. An old crone came to prepare their dinner, but there was no fire made and no kindling or wood to be seen.

"I will go and find some kindling and chop some wood for you, if you untie me," said the old man. The woman foolishly did not suspect anything. She let the old man go free. He went out and found a big stick. Back he ran into the house where the crone waited.

"This is how I chop wood," cried the old man, and he whacked the woman on the legs so that she fell down. He ran into the house, collected the parrot, and returned to the nobleman's house. The nobleman was so pleased to see his parrot again that he rewarded the old man with a lot of money. The old man was never hungry again.

But when the two rascals returned to their hut and saw the woman lying down and the third rascal asleep, they were furious. They took the sleeping rascal, put him in a barrel in which they had left only one small hole, and rolled the barrel far into the forest. Sure enough, a wolf came along and sniffed at the barrel. It tried to put its snout into the hole, but it did not fit. The wolf then put its tail into the hole. The rascal inside grabbed hold of the wolf's tail. The wolf howled and pulled the barrel along until it broke into pieces. Before the wolf could recover, the third rascal fled. He gave up thieving and never returned to his companions, but made his living in honest ways. But I don't know about the other two rascals. They may still be around trying to steal from you.

THE FIVE CLEVER GIRLS

There are variants of this type of story in many countries. In most cases it is only one girl who outwits a trickster by riddling. Here it is five sisters. When telling this to young children, it is entertaining to use a set of nesting dolls.

*T*here was once a trickster named Gonella, who made his living by tricking people. He would go from town to town and always had enough to eat and coins in his pocket, without lifting a finger to work.

One day Gonella was coming to a small village in Poland where he had never been before. At the edge of the village he saw a small house, and in front of it was a young girl. She did not look too bright, so Gonella was sure he could trick her or someone in her family.

"Good day, Panna," he said politely. "Where is your father?"

"Good day, sir," she answered just as politely. "My father is busy. He is busy making many out of few." Gonella did not understand this answer, but he did not say so out loud. He just turned around to see if there was someone else in the family he could trick. At that moment, from behind the girl stepped her younger sister.

"Good day, Panna! Where is your mother?" asked Gonella.

"Good day, sir! My mother is busy. She is busy making something better out of something good." Gonella did not understand that answer either. But he was not about to admit it.

Just then, from behind the two girls stepped a still younger sister. Gonella addressed her just as politely and asked, "Where is your older brother?"

"Good day, sir! My older brother is busy. He is busy hunting between heaven and earth."

Are these girls trying to trick me? thought Gonella. He decided he had better go on to another house in the village. But just then a very small girl stepped out from behind the third sister. She was quite small. Gonella felt she would surely give an answer he could understand. After greeting her politely he asked, "Where is your grandfather?"

"Good day, sir!" she answered. "My grandfather is busy. He is busy closing the door to keep it open."

These girls are answering me with riddles, thought Gonella. He decided to go on to the next house. At that moment the baby of the family stepped out from behind her sisters. She could just barely talk.

"I might as well ask her something," said Gonella to himself. He approached the little girl and in a baby-talk voice said, "Hello there, little one. You will surely tell me where your grandmother is, won't you?"

"Granny is busy," said the little girl. "She is busy baking bread we've already eaten."

That was too much for Gonella. He shouted at the girls: "You are all naughty. Why are you telling me all those lies?"

"Oh, no, sir! It's the truth," cried the little girl. "Can't you smell?"

Gonella sniffed. He did smell bread breaking. But how could it be bread they had already eaten? All of the girls rushed to give an explanation.

"Yesterday, Granny saw we had no more bread in the house."

"She sent us to the neighbor to borrow five loaves."

"That evening, we were so hungry we ate them all."

"This morning, Granny set about baking her usual five loaves of bread."

"As soon as they were in the oven she said, 'My goodness! I forgot we had to pay back five loaves to the neighbor. I'm baking bread we've already eaten.' "

What a clever answer for such little girls, thought Gonella. But he said nothing aloud. He thought he had better find out what the other answers meant, so no one could trick him with them. He went to the next oldest girl and asked, "What did you mean when you said your grandfather was closing the door to keep it open?"

She pointed to a spot by the river. "There is Grandfather, mending the fish net in which we keep the fish we are going to eat some day. Yesterday, one of the fish made a big hole in the net. Grandfather said it was like a door letting out the other fish. So he had to close that door. But he did not want to close it so tightly that the fish could not move around. So Grandfather said he had to close the door just enough to still keep the net open."

"What was that about your brother? How could he hunt between heaven and earth?" Gonella asked the next girl.

"There he is," cried the girl, pointing up a tree. "He's up in the cherry tree, hunting for the sweetest cherries. He's not up in heaven. He's not on earth. He's hunting between heaven and earth."

Gonella went to the next oldest girl and asked, "What did you mean about your mother making something better out of something good?"

"Listen," she said "and you will hear the thumping of her churn. She is making butter out of cream. Cream is good, but butter is better."

"I would have figured it out if you had let me listen a bit longer," said Gonella. "But what was that about your father making many out of few?"

Are you smarter than Gonella? Can you figure out what her father was doing?

"He is planting seeds," said the oldest girl. "For every hundred seeds he plants, he will harvest a thousand. He is making many out of few."

"Well," said Gonella to himself, "if the children around here are so clever, what must the grown-ups be like? I don't think I will have any luck tricking them." And he turned around and left that part of Poland, and never returned.

And that's how five clever girls saved their village from being tricked by Gonella.

THE STORK AND THE DUCK

This is the type of story in which a physical action is part of the ending—in this case, the tweaking of a nose. It also depends on the play of words, so it might be a good idea to explain that trzos, the Polish word for money bag, can also be the slang word for stomach.

*O*ne day a stork was walking through a village and he met a duck. The stork suggested that the duck should come along with him.

"Oh, I cannot travel now," replied the duck. "Easter is coming, and my mistress needs my eggs. If I don't lay eggs for her, she will not give me any food."

"You lay eggs for someone else?" exclaimed the stork. "I would never do that. Why don't you come along with me? You would do much better in life." In the end, the stork convinced the duck to go along.

They walked and walked, through a forest and down many paths. Finally they arrived at an inn. The stork wanted to charm the duck and show off, so he invited her in to have a fine meal. When they had finished, the innkeeper demanded payment. But neither the stork nor the duck had any money. So the owner shut them up in his kitchen for the night.

The next morning the innkeeper came in to the kitchen and saw that the duck had laid an egg, a nice big one.

"I will put this egg with the eggs of the mother hen. It will hatch out, and I will have a nice duck. In the end, that will make a fine meal for several people. It is enough payment for your meal, duck." He let the duck go free.

The stork was very unhappy. "How come you let the duck go, but you keep me a prisoner here?" The innkeeper said he would let the stork go if he could find some method of payment. He again left the stork in the kitchen, but he kept his eye on the stork to see what he would do. The stork opened his beak very wide—you could have looked right down into his stomach, which still contained all the food he had eaten the day before.

"What are you doing?" asked the innkeeper.

"I am just checking on my money bag," replied the stork. Now when the innkeeper heard what the stork said, he decided he wanted to see if the stork had a money bag in his stomach. He went up to the stork and put his eye right next to the stork's beak . . . .

[Here, the storyteller pauses for quite a while, saying nothing, and someone in the audience will usually ask, "What happened?" The storyteller responds by twisting gently the nose of the one who asked the question.]

PART 8

Why Tales

TWO BRAIDS

Whether this tale is based on factual events or not, it is true that most married women in Poland did wear their hair in such a fashion until well into the twentieth century

*I*n the Vistula River area, near the town of Gora Kalwaria, there lived a very unhappy couple. They wanted very much to have children, but each time the wife gave birth to a child, it died soon after. Finally they made a pilgrimage to St. Anthony. On their way home, they met a poor man asking for food. The wife shared what food they had, and then told her sad story.

The old man said, "When you are ready to deliver your next child, you must send your husband to the top of the dike that is by the river. He must call out in exactly this way: 'Grandfather Anthony, please come to us'."

The husband and wife promised they would do this. Some months later the wife bore a son, and the husband went to the dike and called out as he had been told to do: "Grandfather Anthony, please come to us." Sure enough, the old man appeared. That night, while the wife slept, he watched the baby. Death and an Angel both came, ready to take the soul of the little child, but Grandfather Anthony began to talk to them and ask them questions. Finally, he asked them outright if they could spare the life of this baby.

Death agreed, on one condition. The boy would live only up to the day of his wedding, and then he would drown in the Vistula River. Death left and the Angel said, "You must tell the parents to call you on the boy's wedding day, just as they called to you at his birth. And you must remember the mercy of God."

When the parents awoke, the old man said, "You must call to me again on the morning of the day your son is to be married. I *must* be present at his wedding."

The happy parents promised they would do so. The boy grew up and developed into a handsome young man. He fell in love with a shy, sweet girl who was known by everyone for her kind and generous heart. She lived across the river from the town where the young man lived. On the morning of the wedding, the party set off in a horse and carriage to fetch the bride, as was the custom in Poland at that time.

Suddenly the parents remembered what the old man had said, so the father went out to the dike and called, "Grandfather Anthony, come to us." Once again the old man appeared. He took his place at the side of the son. During the trip he did not leave him for one moment, especially during the crossing they had to make on the small ferry across the river. This ferry was simply a platform of wood, guided by a stout rope.

The bridegroom and his party made the crossing with no trouble. On the return to the church where the wedding was to be held, the ferry, with the horse and carriage on it, had to cross against the current. It was choppy and the ferry bobbed up and down. When it bobbed low on the side where the horse was tied up, the tail of the horse dipped into the water. The horse, surprised, flicked his tail, and the water sprinkled all over the young bridegroom. The young man fell over in a swoon and looked as though he were dead.

The family began weeping and wailing, not knowing what to do. Grandfather Anthony called on Death and the Angel. "You must not let this happen," he cried. Death refused to change. He was going to take the young man, as he had foretold. The Angel said, "Remember the mercy of God. The bridegroom will be returned to life if there is someone who will share his lifespan with him. That person must agree to live exactly as long as this young man."

Grandfather Anthony went to the parents, but they were too confused to consider what they were saying, and both refused. The bride, who had been weeping quietly, said, "I will divide my life with him in the same way I have divided my hair, by parting it down the middle and making two braids, one on each side of my head."

At the moment she said this, the young bridegroom sat up and was alive and well. They went ahead with the wedding, and the couple lived to a ripe old age.

From that time on, in that part of Poland it was customary for married women to part their hair in the middle and wear it in two braids, twined in circles on each side of the head. It was a symbol that each was willing to share her life with her husband.

WHY THE BEE MAKES HONEY AND THE WASP HAS A STING

*J*esus and John were walking along one day, when they came to a town celebrating a church fair. They followed along with the other pilgrims. They had only bread crusts to eat. Now John was hungry and wanted to eat some bread without Jesus's knowledge. He tried to eat the crust of bread silently, but it was so dry that each bite he took made a loud crunching noise. Disgusted, he threw the rest of the bread crust away. A crumb of the dried bread hit Jesus in the forehead and caused a tiny drop of blood to form where the crust broke the skin.

Jesus was saddened at John's action, but he simply touched his forehead and said, "Out of my pain will come sweet solace." The bread crumb turned into a bee. The drop of blood turned to honey.

The devil saw this and said, "I can do the same thing." He threw a piece of hard, dried bread at his forehead. The bread turned into a wasp. The place where the bread hit his forehead started to swell because in it was the sting of the wasp.

THE AGES OF MAN

This was one of the many stories told by Sabala in Zakopane, in the late 1800s. He was one of the few Polish tellers of that century whose entire repertoire was taken down. According to the original text, Sabala would end most of the important sentences with a "hey," as if to make his audience pay particular attention.

*A*fter God created the animals, he called to the lion and said, "I will rule over the humans, but you will be the ruler of all the animals." When the animals heard this, they were not happy. Ox, donkey, calf, and dog got together and started to discuss how they could get rid of lion as the ruler. Each secretly thought, "I will be ruler."

The four animals began to spread the word that lion was not the best ruler. They should look for some other animal. Dog spread the news by barking in various ways, as though he were sending telegrams. Calf bleated as though it was always hungry. Ox bellowed along behind calf, to show he had a stronger voice than lion. Donkey just hee-hawed, raised and lowered his ears, and stubbornly did the exact opposite of what the lion asked him to do.

Lion called the animals together and asked them, "Why are you causing me so much trouble? Who started this? Do you think I am happy being given this job? God told me to take it on, and I had to obey. I will have to punish you all for your silly antics."

"It is ox, donkey, calf, and dog who put us up to this," said the other animals. "They started it."

After lion thought about how he could punish the four of them, he decided he did not want to do it himself. It would dirty his paws and make him look untidy. He had to keep up his looks as a ruler. Instead, he ordered donkey to eat dog, ox to eat donkey, and calf to eat ox. So donkey ate all of dog except the head and skin, ox ate all of donkey except the head and skin, and calf started to eat ox. But calf's teeth were not well-developed yet, and ox's bones were hard. So lion had to finish the job, but he also left the skin and head. Then he buried the skins and heads.

Came the day when God created Man. He searched for some clay, but unfortunately he looked in exactly that spot where the skins and heads of those four animals were buried. And that is why Man, even the cleverest of them, has some qualities of those beasts. When young, he is as stupid as a calf. As a youth, he chases like a dog and won't settle down. When he marries, he works like an ox. And when he is old he is as stubborn as a donkey.

But only men are like that because women were created later!

WHY HORSES ARE ALWAYS HUNGRY

God was walking along beside a river and met horse and ox. He wanted to test them.

"I must get across the river right now. Horse, please take me across."

"Wait a moment," neighed horse. "I haven't eaten much yet today. I need to eat more before I can take you across."

God was angry and said, "If that is how it is now, that is how it will always be. You will always be a little bit hungry before you are asked to go off and do something."

God then turned to ox, "Please, will you take me across the river right now?"

Ox nodded his head, lowered it, and said, "Climb on my back and off we'll go."

From that day on, ox always seems to be ready to work, slowly but surely, and he appears to be well fed at all times. But horse always wants to eat something before it goes off to work, because it is always hungry.

WHY THE WOLF HATES THE DOG, THE DOG HATES THE CAT, AND THE CAT HATES MICE

There are countless tales about why there is enmity between dogs and cats, found in virtually all parts of the world, but this version is very Polish, with its insistence that the animals had their own papers of nobility. It is a perfect reflection of the deep respect for guarding precious papers, especially papers showing even a touch of petty nobility, common in the nineteenth century.

*L*ong ago, all the animals were happy and lived together peacefully. The horses were not bridled, the oxen were not harnessed, and dogs did not serve humans. Even sheep and pigs were free to roam about as they pleased, trying to stay away from human places. Only the cat liked to slink around human homes, searching for a tasty bit to eat or to hear interesting news. It would then run off to the animals in woods and fields and brag about what it knew.

Now, all the animals had their family pedigrees written on parchments and sealed with wax. On the parchments were given their coats of arms and their proper names and titles. The animals guarded these documents with great care. They knew that if they lost them, they would lose their freedom.

Every now and then the parchments would get wet from floods. This disturbed the animals so much, they got together and discussed what to do. Finally it was agreed that they would all be given to one animal whose duty it would be to keep them safe. The dog said, "Why not let the cat do it? He is sly and knows his way among humans. He seems to be up on all they are doing." The animals finally agreed and asked the cat to guard their documents.

The cat simply said, "I will think about it."

The animals began to beg the cat. The cat said it would give an answer in three days. When the day arrived, he said rather haughtily, "I'll agree to do it for the good of the community."

The animals all brought their parchments. It was agreed that after a year they would come to check them out, to see if they were safe. The cat, with the help of the dog, carried the parchments to a corner of a storeroom in the house of one of the humans he frequently visited. He remembered an old chest that was there, standing empty. The cat placed the documents in the chest. At first he checked up on them every so often, but then he forgot about them.

When the year was up, the wolf and the dog, on behalf of the other animals, came to check and see if the parchments were safe. The cat led them to the chest in the storeroom. They bent over to open the chest, and suddenly there was a squeaking and rattling. The moment the chest was open, small shreds of parchment scattered here and there, like dust. The wolf, dog, and cat saw an army of mice scurrying away. They reached into the chest to take out their parchments, but all that was left were more scraps. The mice had chewed up every one. Their documents were lost, and so was their freedom.

"You were supposed to guard them!" barked the dog at the cat. The cat took a leap and jumped up to the rafters and then out on to the roof.

"You were the one that told us to trust the cat," howled the wolf. "It was your advice that got us into this situation. Now get us out." The dog ran and hid under a bench by the human's house.

The man, who was standing there, said, "Well, have you come to join us, like the cat?" And he smiled. He took a club and went after the wolf, telling him to stay away from his place or he would beat him to death. The wolf put his tail between his legs and ran off to the forest.

After that, gone was all peace and harmony among the animals. They had lost their freedom, and many turned against each other. The sheep grew afraid of the wolf and ran to the man for protection, followed by the oxen and the horses. The man was very happy and immediately put them to work, and trained the dog to watch over them.

But the dog could never forgive the cat. Every time he saw him, he would bark at him, "You took them. It was your fault." The cat knew he was guilty and always ran from the dog, jumping up into trees or to the roof of the house. The cat was furious at the mice. He would watch for hours at homes, waiting to catch one and take out his revenge.

And that is how, over the years, the wolf came to hate the dog, the dog came to hate the cat, and the cat came to hate mice.

WHY FEBRUARY IS A SHORT MONTH

*O*ne year the month of March invited February to have dinner with him, but to wait for thirty days. February consulted May and asked her, "How should I go to the dinner with March?"

"You must start your trip in a carriage or cart, but be sure to take along a sleigh, a boat, and a cat," answered May.

February did not know how long the journey would take. He set out in a fine carriage, but it was too soon. March saw February coming and began to let down a thick snowstorm. February transferred to the sleigh and continued on his way. But it was still too early. March unleashed a cloudburst and the land was covered with water. February transferred to the boat and continued on. February reached March's courtyard, but it was still too early. March sent out dogs to bark in warning. February answered by letting the cat out of the boat. The dog ran off to chase the cat, which made February arrive two days too soon.

Since that time, March has been angry with May for giving that advice to February. March threatened May, saying, "I'll put frost on your leaves and buds just when they are ready to come out."

May did not like being threatened. "You are a fool if you think you can harm me. When I draw near, everything melts away and warms up." April heard this, and though she usually followed May, now she decided to follow March, ahead of May. She was the only one who could get along with March, because once when March ran out of days, she loaned him one of hers. And ever since then, the months are like that.

WHY THERE ARE ICE FLOWERS ON WINDOWS IN WINTER

When God created the world, the last things to be created were the flowers. There were so many beautiful flowers in heaven that it was impossible to get them all set out by the end of the sixth day. The most important were the flowers that had to appear on fruit-bearing plants, because if they did not appear, there would be no fruit.

When the needle-bearing trees and plants saw they had no flowers, they complained to God. So God ordered that there should be different seasons. During the warm seasons, most of the trees and plants would be bare, but the needle-bearing ones would remain fresh and green all winter long.

But there were still some small flowers left, and they were sad at being left behind. So God ordered that they could come down during the coldest days of winter and decorate the window panes in homes and churches and other buildings. Since that time, on cold days these flowers come down from heaven, like stars and sit on windows so that we can enjoy their beauty.

PART 9

Religious Legends

SAINT MAGDALENE
AND THE DIKE

*S*aint Magdalene was sent to Nowe Miasto, near the Pilica River in Poland, to do penance. She sat in the mud along the river and refused to leave. The King offered her a fine place to live, and gold besides. But this offer of riches did not tempt her.

One year Magdalene suspected that heavy rains would soon cause a flood over the town of Nowe Miasto. With her own hands, she began to build a high dike all along the river. Sure enough, before long the river flooded, but the people in Nowe Miasto were saved because of the dike, while up and down the river other towns were flooded. This caused the local people to have a special place in their hearts for Magdalene, and they prayed to her often. If they saw a strange light in the sky, they knew that a flood threatened. They knew they must always check the dike, to be sure it was strong enough to withstand any flood.

Centuries passed, and in a more recent year, the light was seen in the sky. The old people in the town warned that a great flood was coming and they must check the dikes. But the young administrator of the town refused to believe in this old legend and just laughed at the superstitious old ones.

A huge flood came, and no one, not even Saint Magdalene, could save the town. The water poured over the broken dike and covered the surrounding area.

WHEN JESUS TRAVELED THROUGH MAZOVIA

A long time ago the people of Mazovia were very rich and lacked for nothing. One day Jesus came to Mazovia dressed as a poor man. He came to the first village on a Sunday. He passed by the church and saw that it was empty. He passed by the tavern and saw that it was full. He stamped his foot, and the empty church crumbled into dust.

He passed through the second village and asked for something to eat. No one would give him any food. He saw a woman with a baby. She had just fed the baby and was using a slice of bread to clean the baby's face. Jesus asked her for the bread, but she would not give it to him.

He went to a third village and at the edge of the village saw a man making a fence of straw. "Why are you making your fence of straw?" asked Jesus. "Surely it will be too weak to hold up to anything."

"Why should I make it stronger?" asked the man. "I have a disease, and tomorrow I will die." The man was too angry to share anything.

Jesus kept walking, but by now he was very weak. He fell down on a large rock, but the rock immediately turned soft so as not to hurt him. On the spot where Jesus fell were left five marks. An old woman was passing, and she took pity on him. She brought bread and soup and a boiled egg and gave them to him to eat. Jesus regained his strength and left, blessing her and all who lived in the village.

When the other villagers heard about this, they decided to bring bread and eggs and other food to the spot where the rock was. Soon poor people from all around knew that if they came to that place, they could always get a bit of food. In the middle of the nineteenth century, a new priest came and wanted to build a bigger church. He ordered the stonemasons to carve up the rock. But the people protested and insisted that some of the rock must stay in place. They built a small shrine around it and put a statue inside. The statue has a blue mantle and scarf. People who are sick come and touch the statue and rub the scarf over their skin, eyes, or whatever part of their body ails them. And to this day, food is left at the shrine so that if you are hungry, you can come and take something to eat.

View of the interior of the chapel. Photo by Michał Malinowski

OUR LADY OF CZESTOCHOWA

This shrine, at Jasna Gora Monastery at the edge of the city of Czestochowa, is the most beloved in all of Poland. Many thousands make a pilgrimage there every year. There are so many legends connected to the icon of the Madonna and Child that it is difficult to sort them out. Here we have tried to include those that have been told orally or read for at least several hundred years. To the best of our knowledge, the icon has never been scientifically dated, but the legend is that it was painted by St. Luke, on a tabletop made of cypress wood, a table that was once used in the home of Jesus, Mary, and Joseph.

A long time ago, in the year 1382, a beautiful icon of Mary and the child Jesus traveled from Jerusalem to Constantinople, and from there to the monastery of Jasna Gora, in Czestochowa. Some say it was during this journey that those carrying the icon were attacked. To protect it, they buried it in deep mud, and when they unearthed it and cleaned it, the Madonna and Child had black skin. Others say that the blackness came from a fire caused by one of the many invasions of fierce tribes who plagued all the countries in that region in the Middle Ages. It could have happened, they say, either before the icon came to Poland, or after it was there.

When the Hussites attacked the monastery in the fifteenth century, one of the Hussite men drew his sword and slashed the painting two times. Some say that when he tried to strike it a third time, he fell over dead. Others say that the painting began to bleed and the Hussite fled in terror. No matter how they tried to mend the painting on wood, the marks remained.

More than 200 years later, in the middle of the seventeenth century, the Swedish King Gustavus Adolphus decided to gain control of all the lands surrounding the Baltic Sea. His troops occupied the northern part of Poland for some years. Then they began to move farther into Poland. But they could not get beyond Czestochowa, for the Black Madonna miraculously prevented it. King Jan Kazimierz crowned Our Lady of Czestochowa in Lwow, on April 1, 1656. She was declared Queen and Protector of Poland, and has retained this title ever since.

SAINT STANISLAUS
AND THE WOLF

This is reminiscent of the stories told about Saint Francis of Assisi. It may well be that the tale was simply an adaptation of the medieval legend of Saint Francis and the wolf, except that in this case, the wolf does not reform.

One day Saint Stanislaus was walking through a forest and he came upon a wolf, caught by his tail in a trap. The wolf could have escaped, but it would have torn off most of his magnificent, bushy tail. He was very proud of it. Saint Stanislaus greeted the wolf kindly, and the wolf decided to ask the saint for a favor.

"I have tasted stag, lamb, goat, sheep, venison, and horse. But I have never once tasted human flesh. They say it is sweet. Will you let me go free and tell me a way in which I can taste it just once?"

"You'll be sorry," said Saint Stanislaus sadly.

"No, I promise you, I won't. Just let me satisfy my curiosity."

"All right. I will permit you to eat a human being. But there are conditions. You may not eat a child going to or from school. You may not eat an old person with white hair. In fact, the only person you will be allowed to taste is a blacksmith. If you agree to this condition, I will free your tail and you can be on your way."

The wolf agreed and went to the side of the road to wait. Some children came along, walking home from school. An old man passed by, leaning on his cane. The wolf began to get hungry. Suddenly he saw a young man walking toward him on the road, whistling a tune.

"Who are you?" asked the wolf.

"I'm a blacksmith. I work with a will for anyone who needs me. Why are you sitting here, wolf?"

"I have been waiting for you to come along. Saint Stanislaus gave me permission to taste human flesh, but only if it belonged to a blacksmith."

"Hmm," said the blacksmith. "Are you sure you would not prefer a tasty bit of lamb?"

"No, I know how lamb tastes. I only want a taste of human flesh."

"All right," said the blacksmith. "But let me wash myself first in that river there. As you see, I am covered in soot, and that would hide the taste of my flesh."

"Very well," said the wolf. "But I am going to watch you closely. Don't think you can get away."

The blacksmith washed himself in the river and secretly cut a stout stick from one of the trees hanging over the water.

"I'm ready," he called to the wolf. "Just turn to me with your bushy tail facing me, so I can dry myself on it. It is a really superb tail."

The wolf turned around so that his tail was right in front of the blacksmith. The blacksmith seized the tail and wound it around his arm three times, then began to beat the wolf with the stick. The wolf lay there, not dead, but completely knocked out.

The blacksmith continued on his way, whistling merrily.

When the wolf came to his senses, he barely managed to get up. He did not even remember how he had fallen down. He ached all over. He began to moan and groan. Saint Stanislaus heard him.

"What's the matter?" he asked.

"I am sick. I tried to eat blacksmith, but human flesh is bitter."

"Is it really as bad as all that?"

"Yes," said the wolf. "I'm never going near a human again."

And that is why, in Poland, wolves never go near humans.

PART 10

Supernatural Creatures

SUPERNATURAL CREATURES

In this section are brief descriptions of some of the supernatural creatures that are often mentioned in personal experience tales told in Poland. Personal experience tales almost always describe something that happened to another person, who told it to the current teller, who is simply passing it on. They are invariably presented as true stories.

Boruta is a well-known demon, gray in color, that sits in the ruins of a castle in Leczyca. It is long-lived and survives for centuries. It is also known to appear in the lower crypts of some cathedrals. It is often surrounded by owls, and even takes that shape. However, it can also take the shape of an old nobleman, or the wind, or a ghostly figure that is human or animal. Boruta has had a particular resonance with young Poles of today because of several artistic depictions, most notably the animated film by Bartosz Nowakowski.

Dziwozona are naughty spirits who like nothing better than to exchange a real child with a spirit child that looks the same. The real child is usually stolen from a crib and the parents suddenly begin to notice the strange behavior of the child put in its place. To find out if it is a spirit child, one must boil some food with eggshells and then mash it and feed it to the child. If it is a spirit child, it will eat the mixture.

Geometra is the spirit of someone who measured land dishonestly. The spirit appears in the form of fire that passes over the fields and is usually visible from late afternoon to late evening. This fire was very widespread throughout the second half of the twentieth century and has recently reappeared. Some say this is because of the use of modern fertilizers.

Klepaczki are water spirits that appear by the banks of rivers. The name comes from the sound made by the beating of laundry with wooden laundry paddles. The spirits assume the form of washerwomen who have one breast so long it is used as a laundry paddle. They are often accused of tickling men to death or of stealing babies.

Panek is a forest spirit, but also appears on river banks. It guards the forest, bridges, and any spot that affords easy passage. It is good or evil, depending on the person who experiences it. A typical action is stopping a wedding party from crossing a footbridge because there is a dangerous hole or weak spot in it.

Planetnik are huge weather monsters, each with a different function. Some can transform clouds into rain, sleet, or snow. Others cause hail and windstorms. Still others can empty a pond of water by sucking it up into a rainbow. They usually serve evil purposes and often work in conjunction with devils.

Poudnica are whirlwind spirits or dust cloud spirits. They often appear at midday and make people confused and careless from too much sun. They are also known to cut people down with a scythe.

Rusalki (singular, *Rusalka*) are female spirits that usually appear in the forests, lakes, and rivers of Poland. They take different forms and are credited with doing either mischief or harm. *Wilas* are one common type, said to be the beautiful incarnations of dead girls, and are responsible for leading young men astray. Another type are the Sky Women, who were believed to rise from water in the form of small whirlwinds, like tiny tornados. They were also believed to be responsible for certain types of snowstorms in which people lost their way.

Strachy nocne are apparitions or spirits that one encounters when walking home late at night. They often appear as strange dogs, horses, or amorphous white figures. Their usual haunts are under bridges, along secluded roads, and in fields of high, whispering grain or grass.

Strzygon is usually a headless figure carrying its head under an arm. It often visits people in lonely country houses, to help a woman in labor or a sick person in the house.

Topielec is a water demon who calls people to the swamp and pulls them in. It also takes hold of persons who drown accidentally. When someone comes to recover the body, it tries to pull that person down as well.

Wyprawa na Sabat is a description of an event such as an orgy of devils or a meeting of witches that one views as though in a dream. It usually takes place in a swampy area. When one wakes up, one is often in the place where the event dreamed about took place, but all the devils and/or witches and their paraphernalia have disappeared. Often it is impossible to find one's way back to safety or home.

Zmora is a creature that attacks one while sleeping. One has the constant feeling one is choking, or that a heavy weight is pressing on one's chest. It is believed that the *zmora* can be called up by a human person, especially one who is jealous because of the money or position enjoyed by the neighbors. The *zmora* can instantly change form, so that if one awakens quickly and tries to catch the figure, it turns into something like an apple or a nut. The *zmora* seems to be known among Polish Americans as well. Catherine Ainsworth, in her book *Polish-American Folktales* (p. 52), mentions a story told by a woman living in Buffalo, New York, in which a *zmora* turns into an apple, and the person who was molested by the *zmora* cuts the apple and thus gets rid of the *zmora*.

SOURCES

Sources of the Stories

Sources are cited here by the author's last name only, as well as the first word of the title if there is more than one source by that author. Complete bibliographic information can be found in the "Bibliography." Those items taken directly from oral sources by either of the authors of this book are identified with MM for Michał Malinowski and AP for Anne Pellowski. The tale types mentioned come from *The Types of the Folktale* by Antti Aarne and Stith Thompson. If no tale type is given, it was not possible to locate one close enough to the types given in Aarne and Thompson. The motifs are from the classification given in *Motif-Index of Folk-Literature* by Stith Thompson.

Part 3

Lech, Čech, and Rus. Motifs include J50, wisdom acquired from observation, and J680, forethought in alliances. This is a version told orally by AP for several decades. It was learned from an oral telling in Poland in the 1950s, and a few points were checked in the brief mention in Kadłubek's *Kronika Polska* (often cited in English as *The Chronicle of Poland*), probably written down about 1200.

King Popiel. Type 747A. It has the motif B268.6, an army made up of mice, as one of the key elements. This is adapted from the brief description by the anonymous monk known as Gallus Anonymous, who wrote what is acknowledged to be the first history of Poland, sometime between 1112 and 1116 C.E. It is the source of many stories that are more legendary than historically provable, the source for many Poles of many beliefs and theories about the founding of early Poland. There are also some elements taken from Baszko in his work, generally known in English as the *Chronicle of Greater Poland*. Other forms of the name Popiel are Popel and Pumpel, but Popiel is the most widely accepted one.

The Founding of the Piast Dynasty. Type 750. The motifs of the pitcher supplying endless amounts to drink, D1472.1, and a table or tablecloth giving endless supplies of food, D1472.1.7ff, are very ancient. This also was adapted from the brief mentions in Gallus Anonymous, as well as Kadłubek.

The Dragon of Wawel. Type 300. It has motifs similar to those found in H1174.2, in which the task is to kill a dragon. Another motif is B11.11.10, in which a dragon is fed something that makes it drink until it explodes. The version given here has been retold from many sources, the earliest being Kadłubek and Baszko.

Queen Wanda. Type 1468. Motif J2463.2 concerns a girl who complains of being forced to marry a stranger. Wanda is one of the key figures in early Polish legends. There are some who believe that the Vandals were early Poles, and that they took their name from Wanda, which is pronounced Vanda. This is adapted from the mentions in the early chronicle of Baszko and from short versions given in Kromer and the article by Kruszewska.

The Trumpeter of Krakow. A motif included in the story is D1317.9.1, in which the trumpet of a statue warns that a stranger is approaching the city. The first mention of the trumpet call in Krakow comes from a document dated 1392. This is adapted from the oral version of MM and from the same details mentioned in numerous books.

The Warsaw Mermaid. This has as its key motif D1719.7, the magic power of a mermaid. The origins of the two tales are unknown. It is known that the first version of the crest appeared in 1390, and the first modern depiction, as it is shown now, was in 1622. This is based on oral versions of MM and many other Poles of Warsaw, most of whom know at least one version of the legend.

Bazyliszek. Motifs include H1174.2 and other dragon motifs. According to Krzyżanowski (*Polska*), this is based on an episode in the life of Alexander the Great and somehow got transplanted into Poland, where it was affiliated with an actual house in Warsaw. This is translated and slightly adapted from Zahorski. It is also found in Zmorski, Kolberg, and many other sources.

The Sleeping Knights. Type 766, soldiers killed in battle fall asleep and awaken when called upon in the future. Some of the motifs included are to be found in the category D1960.2ff, concerning a king asleep in a mountain and horses that must be shod regularly, and also in E502, in which a sleeping army awakens. This is mostly translated from the version by Kasprowicz but includes a few elements by the famous storyteller Sabała, found in the book by Stopka. In other parts of Poland, the army is asleep after the Swedish invasion, or it is the army of St. Jadwiga that was put to sleep after being pushed out of Silesia.

Pan Twardowski. Partly type 802 and partly type 812. There are numerous motifs in various versions of the tale, but the most common are M210 and M211, making a bargain with the devil; G303.16.19.6, in which a man is protected from devil by holding a child; and A751.1, in which a man is put on the moon as a punishment. This is a straightforward translation from the collection by Wójcicki.

Jurata, the Baltic Queen. Some of the motifs that can be compared include F133, the other world under the sea; F 725.3, a palace or castle under the sea; A421.1.1, a sea creature (queen) and her helpers entice men; and B81.2, a mermaid marries a human. This is a direct translation from the version in Siemieński.

Janosik. Krzyżanowski considers this type 8252. Motifs include A526.7, a culture hero who performs remarkable feats of strength and skill, and J1269.8, in which a robber defends stealing from the rich by saying that otherwise the rich would not get to heaven. The magic gifts of shirt and belt are covered under motifs D1056 and D1057. In Polish, the first mention of the Janosik legends is in Wójcicki. This is adapted from that account and from many oral bits and pieces told by many Poles.

Morskie Oko. Type 424. Motifs include T50.2, a king who does not want his daughter to marry, and T381.0.1, in which the king or nobleman puts his daughter in a convent to prevent her from marrying. A911 is about bodies of water created from tears. This combines translations from Wójcicki and Kasprowicz plus oral versions recorded by MM from Józef Budź of Murzasichle.

Sobotnia Mountain. Type 551. There are many common European motifs here, including H1242, in which a youngest brother succeeds in a quest, and H1321.1, in which the search for the water of life takes place and is usually successful. This version includes elements from Zmorski and Kolberg (volume 8) but is also from an oral version collected by MM from Cecylia Słapek of Nowa Słupia.

Part 4

The Righteous Rabbit. Type 38. Motifs include B437.4, about helpful rabbits or hares; J1172.3, about an ungrateful animal that is returned to captivity or a trap; and U10, about justice and injustice. This is a translation from Dygasiński.

The Lone Wolf. Type 122A. Escape through deception (K500), escape by means of pleading that one must first say prayers (K551.1), escape by insisting one must first be allowed to baptize one's children (K551.8), and losing a tail (A2216) are among the motifs included. This is a combination of the versions in Barącz and Lorentz.

The Cat and the Fox. Type 105. Deception through bluffing (K1700) is the key motif here. This is a straightforward translation from Ciszewski.

The Fox and the Fisherman. Type 1. Among the common motifs present here are L315.15, in which a small animal dupes a large one into a trap, and A2216, in which an animal (in this case a wolf) gets its tail caught in ice or a trap. This version combines translations from Koneczna and Pomianowska, and Lorentz.

Mother Owl and the Hawk. Type 247. The motif here is T681, that one likes one's own children best and finds them to be the prettiest. This is translated directly from Ciszewski.

Rabbit Stops Complaining. Type 70. Motifs include A1856, creation of the rabbit or hare; A2200, animal characteristics; and A2461.1, in which the hare sleeps with one eye open as a defense. This is slightly adapted from Kolberg, volume 8.

Part 5

The Flower of the Fern. Type 623. A flower that may only be found on St. John's Day is in motif D965.14. The idea that one can be free in poverty but enslaved by wealth is covered by motif J211. This is mostly from the version of Kraszewski but has a few elements taken from Wójcicki and also volume 15 of Kolberg.

The Glass Mountain. Type 530B. A few of the motifs found in this version: F751, a glass mountain with a castle or person at top; H1114, climbing a glass mountain as a task; H331.1.1, a suitor must climb a glass mountain to win a girl or princess; F813.1.1, golden apples are a prize possession; and D532, transformation by putting on claws of an animal. This is translated directly from Wójcicki.

The Fool Who Searched for Fear. Type 326. Two motifs are key here: H1376.2, the quest to learn what fear is, and H1440, the various tests a person is given to see if he or she shows fear. This version is translated from Zmorski.

Madej's Bed. Type 756B. Beds in the otherworld are found in motif F166.8. J172 is the motif covering repentance that is brought about by knowledge of punishment being readied in hell. Z36.1 is the motif covering rewards one gets for confession of one's sins. This is from a version told to MM by Cecylia Słapek of Nowa Słupia.

The Crown of the Snake King. Types 300B, 672, and 678. Motif B244.1 is concerned with the king of the snakes, and D1011.3.1 covers the magic crown of the snake king. B360 is concerned with animals that are grateful for their rescue. This has many versions, but the one here combines the two found in Kasprowicz and Siemieński.

The Hatchet of Janosik. Motifs include a magical sword (hatchet) buried in a stone and an apple tree with golden apples, F813.1.1. This is adapted from A. J. Gliński.

The Lamb, the Tablecloth, and the Club. Type 563. The principal motif is one in which magic gifts of a table or tablecloth that produces food, an animal that spouts gold, and a club that beats on command are given to one person (D861.1). This is remembered by AP from childhood. It was later found in a shorter version in one of her mother's Polish textbooks, produced by the Worzalla Publishing Company of Stevens Point, Wisconsin. Ceynowa (Kjiku) gives a slightly different version and claims it was extant earlier than the Grimm tale of "The Magic Table, the Gold Donkey, and the Cudgel in the Sack." It can also be found in numerous other Kaszubian sources, such as Gulgowski, Lorentz, and Rabska.

The Forbidden Chamber. Type 313B. One of the most common motifs in European folktales is C611, the room or area in a home or castle that it is forbidden to enter. This version is from the Kujawy district, collected in Kolberg, volume 3.

Majka. Type 923B. Most of the motifs found in this tale relate to H1010, impossible tasks. H934 covers those tasks set by a relative; H982 covers those tasks in which animals help in performing the tasks; H1010 covers impossible tasks; and H1091.2 specifically fits the task of sorting impossible amounts of grain and receiving help from birds. The motif J829.3 treats the victor forgiving the vanquished, and L350 treats the triumph of mildness (or kindness) over violence. This is translated from K. Gliński.

Argelus and the Swans. Type 400. Most of the motifs in this tale relate to quests and tests: H1229.1, a quest to fulfill a promise; H1381.3.1.2, a quest for a bride; and H1229.1, a test to see if one can stay awake while guarding the king's garden. Other motifs include the golden apple, F813.1.1, and the use of swan maidens as guardians of treasure, N572.2. This is translated from Lompa.

Part 6

The Pear Tree. Type 2030. This is typical of the formula tales found in Z0-10 and in the motif including a series of tasks, H941. This is translated from the article by Piątkowska.

Hen and Rooster. Type 2030. Another formula tale of the type noted in Z0-10. The motif that is most important here is the linden tree, because it is one of the most important trees in Polish folklore. The phloem, just inside the bark, was used to make everyday shoes for peasants. This is translated from Piątkowska and cited by Simonides (*Księga*).

Ele Mele Joey. Type 2030. Another of the chain tales found in the Z0-Z10 motifs. This version was translated from the collection made by Pisarkowa. For those wanting to do this in the Polish Yiddish version as it was recorded, here is the text:

> *Ele mele Joski*
> *Szwarce kałe ost dy*
> *Rojte szychelach gejt zy*
> *Ofn bajmele sztajt zy.*
> *Wus tojg ir a bajmele?*
> *Błechtełach cy rajsen.*
> *Wus tojg ir dy blechtelach?*
> *Kijełach cy szmajssen.*
> *Wus tojg ir dy kijełach?*
> *Milechł cy melk'n.*
> *Wus tojg ir milech'ł?*
> *Kinderłach cy gebn'*
> *Wus togg ir kinderłach?*
> *Sztajndełach cy klojben.*
> *Wus tojg ir sztajndełach?*
> *A besmedresz'l sufcybojen.*
> *Wus tojg ir besmedresz'ł?*
> *Tylem'ł cyzug'n.*
> *Wus tojg ir tylem'ł?*
> *Ojlom nabeccy hub'n.*

The Hairy, Horned Goat. This also includes motif Z14, in which a set of phrases is repeated over and over, often in a different voice. It also fits in the category of cumulative tales under Z39.1, in which a goat hides in another animal's den and won't come out. Other motifs include K1700, deception through bluffing, and K1800, deception through illusion. This is adapted from Makuszyński.

Part 7

The Goose with One Leg. Type 1539. One of the oldest motifs recorded is this deception, classified under K402.1. A version is told in Boccaccio's *Decameron*. This particular version was recorded in the Kujawy region by Kolberg, in volume 6.

The Princess Who Would Not Laugh. Type 571. The motif of the suitor who must some-how cause a princess to laugh, H341, is very well known throughout Europe. The Grimm version is usually called "The Golden Goose" and is much longer. This version is translated from Barącz.

The King and the Captain. Type 1920. The motif X900 covers general humor that relies on exaggeration and/or lies, and X907.1 refers to a situation in which a second liar corroborates the lies of the first. Lies about huge cabbages have the motif number X1423.1, and those about remarkable buildings are numbered X1030. This is a translation from Ciszewski. It also appears in Saloni.

Cobbler Kopytko and His Duck Kwak. Type 1535. Among the motifs included in this extended tale are K300, theft and cheating; K331, goods that are stolen while the owner is sleeping; and D1004, the magic power of tears. This is only part of a long cycle, translated and adapted from the version recorded in Makuszyński.

How the Papaje Made a Journey. Type 1200. Numskulls who go on a journey are covered in motif J1711, and J2333 refers to a situation in which carts or carriages are left in the direction one wants to continue on the following morning, only to be turned around during the night by a trickster. This is translated from Rutkowski.

The Very Smart Son. Type 2098. The main motif is J1741.3.3, about the stupid scholar who tries to memorize answers in Latin. This is translated from Ciszewski.

The Inheritance of a Cat. Type 240. The cat as the only thing inherited is covered in motif N411.1.1, and a country without cats is motif F708.1. This is translated from Udziela.

Three Rascals. Type 325. A number of deception motifs are included here, including escape by deception, K500; escape by means of a false plea, K550; and escape because the captor or guard is beguiled, K600. This was recorded by P. Gawel and can be found written down in the Saloni article.

The Five Clever Girls. Type 655 or 875, both concerned with clever riddles. AP has evolved this story from a brief medieval tale mentioned in Wesselski. The riddles were taken from some of the Polish riddles mentioned in De Vries and from oral sources, after much experimentation to determine which worked best in oral storytelling.

The Stork and the Duck. Type 237. This is adapted from Kolberg, volume 14, and was recorded in the Poznań area.

Part 8

Two Braids. One motif is D577, a change brought about by braiding hair. M200 concerns the giving of a solemn promise, and T210 treats faithfulness in marriage. This is from an oral telling to MM by Piotr Makowski of Mlądz, Mazovia.

Why the Bee Makes Honey and the Wasp Has a Sting. The main motif is A2012, the creation of the bee. This version is from an oral telling by Piotr Makowski of Mlądz, Mazovia, as recorded by MM.

The Ages of Man. Type 2462. A basic tale type, a version can be found in one of the fables of Aesop. This has many versions in Poland; the motifs included here are A1200, the creation of man; A1224, parts of man are created from animals; and A1241, man is created from earth. This is a translation of the version told by Sabała, as written down in Stopka.

Why Horses Are Always Hungry. Motif A2500 covers the special characteristic animals have, and A2513 covers why animals serve humans. Although this is known throughout Poland and can be found in many earlier collections, this version was recorded by MM as told by Piotr Makowski of Mlądz, Mazovia.

Why the Wolf Hates the Dog, the Dog Hates the Cat, and the Cat Hates Mice. The chief motif is A2494.1.2, in which the cat loses the certificates of nobility given to the animals and earns the enmity of the dog. This is adapted from several versions recorded by Kolberg and the one by the storyteller Sabała, recorded in Stopka.

Why February Is a Short Month. Type 480B. Motif A1161 includes the reason for February's shorter number of days. This is translated from Kolberg, volume 19.

Why There Are Ice Flowers on Windows in Winter. The origin of flowers is covered in motif A2650, and of magic ice in D904. This is based on an oral telling by AP dating to her work as a storyteller with the New York Public Library in the late 1950s and early 1960s. The source, from the Central Children's Room, could not be located due to materials in the collection being transferred to a new location. There is a brief mention in Benet, giving no source.

Part 9

St. Magdalene and the Dike. This was recorded by MM in a narration by Piotr Makowski of Mlądz, Mazovia.

When Jesus Traveled Through Mazovia. Type 750A. This was also recorded by MM as told by Piotr Makowski of Mlądz, Mazovia.

Our Lady of Częstochowa. This is taken from brief mentions in Długosz and other early sources. It can be told orally by most Poles and was reconstructed here by MM and AP.

St. Stanislaus and the Wolf. Motif B279.1.1, interaction between saint and wolf, is paramount here. This is translated and adapted from Kędzierski. An earlier translation, with more detail, can be found in Bernhard.

Sources of the Nursery Rhymes

These nursery rhymes are extant in many versions in Poland today, both in oral and print forms. These versions are all taken from Rogoszówna (*Sroczka*) and loosely translated by AP. Following are the Polish texts and phonetic pronunciation for the first three rhymes, for Polish Americans who have little or no facility in Polish but wish to include a few of these rhymes when playing with children.

Magpie

Sroczka kaszkê warzyła, (Srotch-ka kash-keh var-zhi-wah)

Dzieci swoje karmiła. (Dzeh-chee svo-yeh kar-mee-wah)

Pierwszemu dała na miseczce, (Pyair-vsheh-moo da-wa no mee-she-cheh)

Drugiemu dała na łyżeczce (Droo-gyeh-moo da-wa na wee-zheh-cheh)

Trzeciemu dała w garnuszeczku (Tcheh-cheh-moo da-wa v gar-nu-shetch-ku)

Czwartemu dała w dzbanuszeczku (Chvar-te-mu da-wa v dzbah-nu-shetch-ku)

A piątemu łeb urwała (Ah pyon-te-mu web ur-va-wa)

I frrrr . . . do lasu poleciała. (Ee frrrr...doh la-su po-lets-ya-wa)

Little Kittens

A – a – a kotki dwa. (Ah, ah, ah, koht-kee dva)

Szaro bure obydwa. (Shah-roh boo=reh oh-bid-vah)

Nic nie będą robiły, (Neets nyeh ben-dah ro-bill-ee)

Tylko _____ bawiły. (Till-koh _____ bah-vill-ee)

Off to Grandma and Grandpa

Tosi, tosi łapci (toh-see, toh-see wop-chee)

Pojedziem do babci (Poh-yeh-jem doh bob-chee)

Babcia da nam mleczka (Bob-cheeya dah nahm mletch-kah)

A dziadzio pierniczka (Ah dzhyah-dzhoo pyair-nitch-kah)

Tosi, tosi łapci (same as above)

Pojedziem do babci. (same as above)

Babcia da nam kaszki, (Bob-cheeya dah nahm kosh-kee)

A dziadzio okraszki (Ah dzhya-dzhyoo oh-krosh-kee)

Sources of the Games and Riddles

The games were taken from personal recollections of MM and from Michalikowa, Piasecki, and Trzesniowski.

The riddles were taken from Gulgowski, Krzyżanowski (Zagadki), and Folfasiński.

BIBLIOGRAPHY

Included here are all works consulted for this book, some only to compare different versions of the tales included. All known collections of Polish tales translated into English are also included. The authors tried to work with original texts, but this was not always possible. For medieval texts and editions published later than the original, the original date of composition or publication is provided in parentheses.

Aarne, Antti, and Stith Thompson. *The Types of the Folktale*. Helsinki: Suomalainen Tiedeakatemia, 1973.

Ainsworth, Catherine Harris. *Polish-American Folklore*. Buffalo, NY: Clyde Press, 1977.

Anstruther, F. C. *Old Polish Legends*. Wood engravings by J. Sekalski. Foreword by Z. Nowakowski. New York: Hippocrene Books, 1991.

Asala, Joanne. *Polish Folklore and Myth*. Iowa City, IA: Penfield Press, 2001.

———. *Polish Proverbs*. Illustrated by Alice Wadowski-Bak. Iowa City, IA: Penfield Press, 1995.

Atlas Polskich Strójów Ludowych. Wrocław, Lublin, Poznań: Polskie Towarzystwo Ludoznawcze, 1949–present.

   Strój Górali Łąckich, ed. Jan Wielek
   Strój Górali Szczawnickich, ed. R. Reinfuss
   Strój Kaszubski, ed. Bożena Stelmachowska
   Strój Kielecki, ed. Aleksandra Jacher-Tyszkowa
   Strój Kolbielski, ed. Władysława Kolago
   Strój Krakówiakow, ed. Tadeusz Seweryn
   Strój Kurpiowski, ed. Maria Żywirska
   Strój Krzczonowski, ed. Janusz Świeży
   Strój Lachów Limanowskich, ed. Jan Wielek
   Strój Lachów Śląskiich, ed. Gustaw Fierla
   Strój Mazowsze I Sieradzki, ed. Jan Piotr Dekowski
   Strój podlaski, ed. Janusz Świeży
   Strój Pomorze I Warmia, ed. Franciszek Klonowski
   Strój Pyrzycki, ed. Agnieszka Dobrowolska
   Strój Rozbarski, ed. Barbara Bazielich

Strój Rzeszowski, ed. Franciszek Klonowski
Strój Szamotulski, ed. Adam Glapa
Strój Wilamowicki, ed. Barbara Bazielich

Barącz, Sadok. *Bajki, fraszki, Podania*. Lwów: Druk A. Wajdowicz, 1886.

Baszko, Godzisław. *Kronika Wielkopolska*. Edited by Brygida Kurbis. Warszawa: Państwowe Wydawnictwo Naukowe, 1965. (Written in approximately 1280–1300.)

Benet, Sula. *Song, Dance and Customs of Peasant Poland*. New York: Roy Publishers, 1951.

Bernhard, Josephine. *The Master Wizard and Other Polish Tales*. New York: Knopf, 1934.

Berwiński, Ryszard. *Studya o gusłach, czarach, zabonach i przesądach ludowych*. Poznań: L. Merzbach, 1862.

Bojar-Fijałkowski, Gracjan. *Pień swantibora: baśnie I Podania Pomorze Zachodniego*. Illustrated by Adam Kilian. Poznań: Wydawnictwo Posnanskie, 1964.

Borkowski, Alfred, and Cezary Leżeński. *Klechdy ciechanowskie*. Warszawa: Epoka, 1980.

Borski, Lucia Merecka. *The Gypsy and the Bear*. New York: Longmans, Green, 1935.

Borski, Lucia Merecka, and Kate B. Miller. *The Jolly Tailor and Other Fairy Tales*. Illustrated by Kazimir Klepacki. New York: Longmans, Green, 1928.

Brzozowska-Krajka, Anna. *Polish Traditional Folklore: The Magic of Time*. Translated by Wiesław Krajka. Boulder, CO: East European Monographs, 1998.

Ceynowa, Florjan. "*Kjiku resze se.*" In *Sto prostonarodnich pohádek a povesti slovanských*, ed. Karel Jaromir Erben. Prague: I. L. Kober, 1865.

———. *Skrb Kaszébskosłovjnskjé móvé*. Świecie: J. Hauffe, 1866.

Chodakowski, Zorian. *Dołęga O słowiańszczyźnie przed chrześcijaństwem*. Warszawa: Państwowe Wydawnictwo Naukowe, 1967. (First published in 1818.)

Chrypiński, Anna. *Polish Customs*. Detroit: Friends of Polish Art, 1977.

Ciszewski, Stanisław. *Krakowiacy. Monografja etnograficzna*. Vol. 1. Kraków: Orbis, 1894.

Czernik, Stanisław. *Klechdy Ludu Polskiego*. Warszawa: Ludowa Spółdzielnia Wydawnicza, 1957.

Czubalowie, Marianna, and Dionizjusz Czubalowie. *Podania i opowieści z zagłębia dąbrowskiego; sto lat temu i dzisiaj*. Katowice: Śląski Instytut Naukowy, Towarzystwo Przyjaciół Opola, 1988.

Dekowski, Jan Piotr. *Strzygi i topieluchy; opowieści Sieradzkie*. Warszawa: Ludowa Spółdzielnia Wydawnicza, 1987.

Długosz, Jan. *The Annals of Jan Długosz*. Translated by Maurice Michael. Chichester, UK: IM Publications, 1997. (Partial translation.)

————. *Ioannis Dlugossii Annales; seu cronicae incliti Regni Poloniae.* Warszawa: Państwowe Wydawnictwo Naukowe, 1964. (Full text in Latin and Polish of work written between 1455 and 1480.)

Dygasiński, Adolf. *Cudowne bajki.* Illustrated by Mieczysław Piotrowski. Warszawa: Czytelnik, 1957. (First published in 1896.)

Dzikowski, Stanisław. *Klechdy polskie.* Warszawa: Józef Kubicki, 1948.

Ficowski, Jerzy. *Sister of the Birds and Other Gypsy Tales.* Translated by Lucia M. Borski. Illustrated by Charles Mikolaycak. Nashville, TN: Abingdon, 1976.

Fijałkowski, Jerzy. *O Zbójach świętokrzyskich.* Staszow: Staszowskie Towarzystwo Kulturalne, 1995.

Folfasiński, Sławomir. *Polskie zagadki ludowe.* Warszawa: Ludowa Spółdzielnia Wydawnicza, 1975.

Gallus Anonymous. *Galli Anonymi Chronicon; Codicis Saeculi XVI Zamoscianus appellati; reproductio paleographica.* Edited by Julian Krzyżanowski. Warszawa: Societas Scientiarum Varsoviensis, 1948. (Reproduction of twelfth-century document, with Polish translation and commentary.)

Gliński, Antoni Józef. *Bajarz Polski.* Wilno: Nakładem W. Makowski, 1899. (First published in 1837.)

Gliński, Kazimierz. *Bajki.* Illustrated by Konstant Górski. Warszawa: Gebethner i Wolff, 1912.

Groome, Francis Hindes. *Gypsy Folk-Tales.* London: Hurst & Blackert, 1899.

Gulgowski, Izydor. *Kaszubi.* Bibljoteka Geograficzna, Series 3, Vol. 2. Kraków: Orbis, 1924.

Jodełka, Tomasz. *Baśnie polskie.* Warszawa: Ludowa Spółdzielnia Wydawnicza, 1957.

Kadłubek, Wincenty. *Kronika Polska.* Translated from the Latin and edited by Brygida Kurbis. Wrocław, Kraków: Zakład Narodowy Imienia Ossolińskich, 1996. (Written about 1200.)

Kapełuś, Helena. *Bajka ludowa w dawnej Polsce.* Warszawa: Państwowy Instytut Wydawniczy, 1968.

Kapełuś, Helena, and Julian Krzyżanowski. *Sto Baśni Ludowych.* Warszawa: Państwowy Instytut Wydawniczy, 1957.

Karasiowa, Anna. *Rozprawki Spod Babiej Góry.* Illustrated by Andrzej Stopka. Kraków: Wydawnictwo Literackie, 1968.

Kasprowicz, Jan. *Bajki, Klechdy i Baśnie.* Vol. 17 of *Dzieła Wybrane.* Kraków: Wydawnictwo Literackie, 1958. (First published in 1930.)

Kędzierski, Czesław. *Bajki polskie wujka Czesia.* Illustrated by Tadeusz Lipski. Poznań: Wydawnictwo Polskie, 1928.

Kędziorzyna, Maria. *Za Siódmą Górą, za Siódmą Rzeką*. Illustrated by Eugenia Różańska. Warszawa: Ksiazka Spółdzielnia Wydawnicza, 1948.

Knab, Sophie Hodorowicz. *Polish Customs, Traditions and Folklore*. Foreword by Czesław Michał Krysa. Illustrated by Mary Anne Knab. New York: Hippocrene Books, 1996.

Kolberg, Oskar. *Dzieła Wszytkie*, 84 vols. Kraków: Polskie Wydawnictwo Muzyczne, 1961–present. (First published 1850s–   ).

Komorowska, Teresa, and Viera Gasparikowa. *Zbójnicki dar; polskie i słowackie opowiadania tatrzańskie*. Warszawa: Ludowa Spółdzielnia Wydawnicza, 1976.

Koneczna, Halina, and Wanda Pomianowska. *Bajki Warmii i Mazur*. Warszawa: Państwowe Wydawnictwo Naukowe, 1956.

Kopernicki, Isidore. "The Wise Young Jew and the Golden Hen." In *Gypsy Folk-tales,* ed. Francis Hindes Groome. London: Hurst & Blackert, 1899.

Krasicki, Ignacy. *Polish Fables: Bilingual Edition*. Translated by Gerald T. Kapolka. Illustrated by Barbara Świdzinka. New York: Hippocrene Books, 1992.

Kraszewski, Józef Ignacy. *Polskie Bajki Ludowe*. Lwów: H. Altenberg, 1884.

Kromer, Marcin. *De Origine et Rebus Gestis Polonorum*. Basel: I. Oporinum, 1558.

Kruszewska, Albina I., and Marion M. Coleman. "The Wanda Theme in Polish Literature and Life." *American Slavic and East European Review* 6, nos. 1–2 (May 1947): 19–35.

Krzyżanowski, Julian. *Paralele; studie porownawcze z pogranicza literatury i folkloru*. Warszawa: Państwowe Wydawnictwo Naukowe, 1977.

———. *Polska Bajka Ludowa w układzie systematycznym*. 2 vols. Warszawa: Zakład Narodowy Imienia Ossolińskich, Wydawnictwo Polskiej Akademii Naukowe, 1962–1963.

———. *Słownik Folkloru Polskiego*. Warszawa: Wiedza Powszechna, 1965.

———. *Szkice Folklorystyczne*. 3 vols. Kraków: Wydawnictwo Literackie, 1980.

———. *W Świecie Bajki Ludowej*. Warszawa: Państwowy Instytut Wydawniczy, 1980.

———. "Zagadka i jej problematyka." *Zagadnienia Rodzajów Literackich* (Łódz) 2–9 (1962): 5–20.

Kulikowski, Mark. *A Bibliography of Slavic Mythology*. Columbus, OH: Slavica Publishers, 1989.

Kumaniecki, K. "Podanie o Wandzie w Świetle Żródeł Starożytnych." *Pamiętnik Literacki* 22–23 (1925–1926): n.p.

Kuniczak, W. S. *The Glass Mountain: Twenty-six Ancient Polish Folktales and Fables*. Illustrated by Pat Bargielski. New York: Hippocrene Books, 1992.

Kupiec, Jan. *Podróż w zaświaty; powieści i bajki Śląskie*. Edited by Dorota Simonides and Jerzy Pośpiech. Illustrated by Elżbieta Murawska. Warszawa: Ludowa Spółdzielnia Wydawnicza, 1975.

Kwaśniewski, Krzystof. *Podania Dolnośląskie*. Wrocław: Wydawnictwo Skryba, 1999.

Leśmian, Bolesław. *Klechdy polskie*. Warszawa: Pax, 1978.

Lompa. Józef. *Bajki i Podania*. Edited by Julian Krzyżanowski, Helena Kapełuś, and Jerzy Pośpiech. Wrocław: Zakład Narodowy Imienia Ossolińskich, 1965. (First published in periodicals from 1843 to 1846.)

Lorentz, Friedrich. *Kaszubi. Kultura ludowa i jezyk*. Toruń: Instytut Bałtycki, 1934.

Makuszyński, Kornel. *Bardzo Dziwne Bajki*. Illustrated by Mikołaj Wisznicki. Warszawa: Gebethner i Wolff, 1929. (First published 1916.)

Michalikowa, Lidia. *Tradycyjne zabawy ludowe*. Warszawa: Centralny Ośrodek Metodyki Upowszechniania Kultury, 1981.

Mikos, Michael. *Medieval Literature of Poland; an Anthology*. New York: Garland, 1992.

Nowak, Zdzisław. *Jak Boruta Zakochał się w Karczmarzowej Córce; baśnie i legendy kurpiowskie*. Illustrated by Jerzy Flisak. Warszawa: Nasza Księgarnia, 1988.

Pan Twardowski: Podania, legendy i baśnie polskie. Edited by Anna Sójka. Illustrated by Andrzej Fonfara. Poznań: Posiędlik-Raniowski i Spółka, 1994.

Pellowski, Anne. *The Family Storytelling Handbook*. Illustrated by Lynn Sweat. New York: Macmillan, 1987.

———. *First Farm in the Valley: Anna's Story*. Illustrated by Wendy Watson. New York: Philomel, 1982. (Paperback eds., St. Mary's Press, 1977; Bethlehem Books, 2008.)

———. *Stairstep Farm: Anna Rose's Story*. Illustrated by Wendy Watson. New York: Philomel, 1981. (Paperback ed., St. Mary's Press, 1998.)

———. *Winding Valley Farm: Annie's Story*. Illustrated by Wendy Watson. New York: Philomel, 1982. (Paperback ed., St. Mary's Press, 1998.)

———. *The World of Storytelling*. 2d ed. New York: H. W. Wilson, 1990.

Perzyński, Włodzimierz. *Wielka Warszawa*. Warszawa: Gebethner i Wolff, 1916.

Piasecki, Eugeniusz. *Zabawy i gry ruchowe*. Warszawa: Polska Towarzysta Nauczycieli Szkól Wyzszych, 1922.

Piątkowska, I. "Cztery bajki z okolicy Sieradza." *Wisła* 17 (1903): 459–61.

Piotrowski, Antoni. *Od Bałtyku do Karpat: Bajki Ludowe*. Kraków: Druk Czasu, 1917.

Pisarkowa, Krystyna. *Wyliczanki Polskie*. Warszawa: Zakład Narodowy Imienia Ossolińskich Wydawnictwo, 1988.

Pokropek, Marian. *Guide to Folk Art and Folklore in Poland*. Translated by Magdalene Mierowska Paszkiewicz. Warszawa: Arkady, 1980.

Poland's Living Folk Culture. Marki, Poland: Parma Press, 2004.

Potocki, Andrzej. *Legendy Łemkowskiego Beskidu*. Rzeszów: Libra, 2007.

Powieści Ludu Krakowskiego. Edited by Mieczysław Karaś. Kraków: Wydawnictwo Literackie, 1959.

Powieści Ludu Orawskiego. Edited by Andrzej Jazowski. Kraków: Wydawnictwo Literackie, 1960.

Powieści Ludu Rzeszowskiego. Edited by Mieczysław Karaś. Kraków: Wydawnictwo Literackie, 1956.

Rabska, Zuzanna. *Baśnie Kaszubskie*. Illustrated by Molly Burkowski. Warszawa: M. Arct, 1925.

Readings in Polish Folklore. Edited by J. B. Rudnyckyi. Winnipeg: University of Manitoba Press, 1953.

Rogoszówna, Zofia. *Koszałki Opałki*. Illustrated by Anna Gramatyki-Ostrowska; Musical arrangements by Stanisława Colonna-Walewska. Warszawa: M. Arct, 1924.

―――. *Sroczka Kaszkę Warzyła*. Illustrated by Zofia Lubańska-Stryjeńska. Lwów: Wydawnictwo Narodowe Imienia Ossolińskich, 1918.

Rutkowski, L. "Gościccy Papaje w Świetle Podań Szlacheckich." *Wisła* 15 (1901): 278–80.

Saloni, A. "Lud Rzeszowski." *Materialy Antropogiczno-Archeologiczne i Etnograficzne* 10 (1908): 242.

Sędzicki, Franciszek. *Baśnie Kaszubskie*. Gdansk: Zrzeszenie Kaszubsko-Pomorskie, Oddział Miejski, 1987.

Seliga, Krzysztof. *Podania I Legendy o Miastach Polskich*. Warszawa: Nasza Księgarnia, 1964.

Siemiński, Lucjan H. *Wieczornice*. Warszawa: Państwowy Instytut Wydawniczy, 1975. (First published in Wilno in 1854.)

Simonides, Dorota. *Księga Humoru Ludowego*. Illustrated by Andrzej Czeczot. Warszawa: Ludowa Spółdzielnia Wydawnicza, 1981.

―――. *Śląskie beranie czyli humor Górnego Śląska*. Katowice: Śląski Instytut Naukowy, Towarzystwo Przyjaciół Opola, 1988.

Simonides, Dorota, and Józef Ligęza. *Gadka za Gadką; 300 Podań, bajek i anegdot z Górnego Śląska*. Katowice: Instytut Śląskii w Opolu, Wydawnictwo Śląskie, 1973.

Sójka, Anna. *Podania, Legendy, Baśnie Polskie*. Illustrated by Andrzej Fonfara. Poznań: Podsiędlik-Raniowski i Spółka, 1995.

Stopka, Andrzej. *Sabała: Bajki; Powiastki; Piosnki; Melodye*. Kraków: L. Zwoliński i Spółka, 1897.

Świrko, Stanisław. *Rok Płaci—Rok Traci*. Poznań: Wydawnictwo Poznańskie, 1990.

Thompson, Stith. *Motif-index of Folk-Literature*. Bloomington: Indiana University Press, 1966.

Trzesniowski, Roman. *Gry i Zabawy Ruchowe*. Warszawa: Wydawnictwo Sport I Turystyka, 1961.

Udziela, Seweryn. *Krakowiacy. Polska, Ziemia i Człowiek*. <u>Biblioteka Geograficzna</u>, Series 3, Vol. 1. Kraków: Orbis, 1924.

Vries, Jan de. *Die Märchen des klugen Rätsellosern*. <u>Folklore Fellows Communications</u>, No. 73. Helsinki: Folklore Fellows Communications, 1928.

Wesselski, Albert. *Die Begebenheiten der Beiden Gonella*. Weimar: A. Duncker, 1920.

Wnuk, Włodzimierz. *Gawędy Skalnego Podhala*. Warszawa: Instytut Wydawniczy Pax, 1960.

Wójcicki, Kazimierz Władysław. *Klechdy, Starożytne Podania i Powieści Ludu Polskiego*. Warszawa: P. Babrycki, 1837.

Wojciechowska, Maria. *Winter Tales from Poland*. New York: Doubleday, 1973.

Zachara-Wnekowa, Antonina. *Baśnie Spod Gorców*. Illustrated by Olga Siemaszko. Warszawa: Ludowa Spółdzielnia Wydawnicza, 1980.

Zahorski, Władysław. *Podania i Legendy Wileńskie*. Wilno: J. Zawadzki, 1925.

Zajdler, Zoe. *Polish Fairy Tales*. Illustrated by Hazel Cook. London: Frederick Muller, 1959.

Zbiór. *Wiadamości do Antropologii Krajowej*. Kraków: Komisja Antropologiczna Akademii Umiejętności. Dział Etnograficzny, 1877–1895.

Zmorski, Roman. *Podania i Baśni Ludu w Mazowszu*. Wrocław: Z. Schletter, 1852.

INDEX

Ferry, 171–72
Festivals, 13
Fiber, 137–39
Fiddle, 24
Finger rhymes, 51, 53
Fire, 135–36
Fisherman, 79–80, 96
"Five Clever Girls, The," 164–66
Floods, 183
"Flower of the Fern, The," 103–6
Flowers, 180
Food, 27–41
Folfasiński, S., 202
"Fool Who Searched for Fear, The," 109–11
"Forbidden Chamber, The," 124–25
Forgiveness, 126–127
"Founding of the Piast Dynasty, The," 63–64
Fox, 90, 95, 141–43
"Fox and the Fisherman, The," 96–97
France, 5, 151
French language, 4, 23
Frogs, 99

Gaels, 5
Gajdy, 24
Galicia, 5
Gallus Anonymous, xi, 194
Games, 42–47
Gawel, P., 199
Gdansk, 8, 11
Geometra, 191
German language, 4, 160–61
Germans, 5, 6
Ghosts, 190–91
Giewont Mountain, 119–21
"Glass Mountain, The," 107–8
Gliński, A. J., 22, 119, 197
Gliński, K., 197
Gniezno, 7, 60, 63
Goat, 92, 135–36, 141–43
God, as character in tales, 99, 135–36, 174–75
Gold, 77
Goose, 93, 147

"Goose with One Leg, The," 147
Goplo, Lake, 61–62
Gora Kalwaria, 171
Goths, 5
Grandparents, 52
Greek Orthodox, 12
Green leaf game, 45
Grimm Brothers, 122, 197
Groome, F. H., 128
Grunwald, battle of, 8
Grupa Studio O, 23
Gulgowski, I., 197, 202
Gustavus Adolphus, 186
Gvjosdkji, 19
Gwiazdki, 19
Gwiazdory, 19
Gypsy tales, 128

Hair, 63–64, 171–72
"Hairy, Horned Goat, The," 141–43
Halas, J., 23
Hanaj, A., photo section
Hanaj, R., photo section
Hanukkah, 20
Harmonica, 126–27
Harvest, 16, 46, photo section
Hatchet, 81, 119–21
"Hatchet of Janosik, The," 119–21
Hawk, 86, 98
Headgear, 13
Hedgehog, 142–43
Hejnal, 68–69
Hen, 137–39
"Hen and Rooster," 137–39
Henry II, Holy Roman Emperor, 8
Henry Valois, Polish King, 9
Hide and seek game, 42
History. *See* Poland, history of
Hohenzollern, Albrecht von, 8
Holidays, 14–19
Holocaust, 6
Holy Cross Mountains, 3, 112–14, photo section
Holy Week, 15
Honey Cake, 38

"Trumpeter of Kraków, The," 68–69
Trzesniowski, R., 202
Turks, 9
Twardowski. *See* "Pan Twardowski"
"Two Braids," 171–72
Types of the Folktale, 193

Udziela, S., 199
Ukraine, 3, 5, 8, 103
Ukrainian language, 4

Vandals, 66, 194
Venison, 35
"Very Smart Son, The," 159
Vienna, battle of, 9
Vienna, Congress of, 10
Virgin Mary. *See* Mary
Vistula River, 3, 8, 65, 67, 171–72
Vistulans, 5

Walesa, L., 11
Wanda. *See* Queen Wanda
Warmia, 96
Warmians, 5
Warsaw, 9–10, 70–71, 72–73
"Warsaw Mermaid, The," 70–71
Warsaw University, 10
Warsaw Uprising, 10
Warta River, 3
Washerwoman, 150
Wasp, 173
Water, 135–36, 137–39
Water of life, 84–86
Water spirits, 190
Wawel, 65
Wax game, 46
Weddings, 17, 24, 47, 117–18, 171–72
Wegrow, 76, photo section
Wesselski, A., 199

"When Jesus Traveled Through
    Mazovia," 184–85
"Why February Is a Short Month," 179
"Why Horses Are Always Hungry," 176
Why tales, 171–80
"Why the Bee Makes Honey and the
    Wasp Has a Sting," 173
"Why the Wolf Hates the Dog, the Dog
    Hates the Cat, and Cats Hate Mice,"
    177–78
"Why There Are Ice Flowers in Winter,"
    180
Wilas, 190
Willow Sunday. *See* Palm Sunday
Wisła. *See* Vistula
Wizard, 124–25
Wojcicki, K., 22, 195, 196
Wojtyla, K. *See* Pope John Paul II
Wolf, 55, 92–94, 96, 163, 177–78, 187–88
Woodcutter, 94
World Wars I and II, 10
Worzalla Publishing Company, 197
Wreaths, 46–47
Wroclaw, 7, 8, 11
Wycinanki, 24
Wyprawa na Sabat, 192, photo section

Yalta Conference, 10
Yiddish language, 198
Yom Kippur, 17

Zahorski, W., 194
Zakopane, 22
Ziemowit, 63–64
Zmora, 192
Zmorski, R., 22, 194, 195, 196
Zocerka, 27
Zurek, 29
Zygmunt. *See* Sigismund

ABOUT THE AUTHORS

Michał Malinowski was born in Warsaw and graduated from the Academy of Fine Arts in Lausanne with a diploma in painting and computer graphics. After working several years in Switzerland and Japan in the field of computer animation, he became interested in folklore, most vividly after a visit to Papua New Guinea, where he observed indigenous storytellers. After studying folklore and mythology at Harvard University for one year, he returned to Poland to found and direct the Storyteller Museum. Since then he has been part of the storytelling revival in Poland and performs throughout Europe. He recently received a UNESCO grant to organize an exhibition and demonstration on West African oral traditions as part of his museum's goal of recording the totality of storytelling performance.

Anne Pellowski was born in Pine Creek, Wisconsin, part of a large Polish American family and community. She served as a children's librarian in the New York Public Library for almost ten years, doing storytelling in most of the branch libraries, and in parks, schools, and playgrounds. She has published a series of novels based on five generations of her Polish American family and has also published *The World of Storytelling,* a comprehensive history, as well as the following story collections: *The Story Vine, The Family Storytelling Handbook, Hidden Stories in Plants, The Storytelling Handbook for Young People, A World of Children's Stories,* and *Drawing Stories from Around the World.* She lives in Winona, Minnesota, but travels frequently to do volunteer work under the auspices the International Board on Books for Young People.

Recent Titles in the
World Folklore Series

The Singing Top: Tales from Malaysia, Singapore, and Brunei
Retold and Edited by Margaret Read MacDonald

Princess Peacock: Tales from the Other Peoples of China
Retold by Haiwang Yuan

Lao Folktales
Kongdeuane Nettavong, Wajuppa Tossa; Edited by Margaret Read MacDonald

A Fire in My Heart: Kurdish Tales
Retold by Diane Edgecomb; with Contributions by Mohammed M.A. Ahmed and Çeto Ozel

The Flying Dutchman and Other Folktales from the Netherlands
Theo Meder

Folktales from the Japanese Countryside
As told by Hiroko Fujita; Edited by Fran Stallings with Harold Wright and Miki Sakurai

Mayan Folktales; Cuentos folklóricos mayas
Retold and Edited by Susan Conklin Thompson, Keith Thompson, and Lidia López de López

The Flower of Paradise and Other Armenian Tales
Translated and Retold by Bonnie C. Marshall; Edited and with a Foreword by Virginia Tashjian

The Magic Lotus Lantern and Other Tales from the Han Chinese
Haiwang Yuan

Brazilian Folktales
Livia de Almeida and Ana Portella; Edited by Margaret Read MacDonald

The Seven Swabians, and Other German Folktales
Anna Altmann

English Folktales
Edited by Dan Keding and Amy Douglas

Additional titles in this series can be found at www.lu.com